MW00777545

Truth Matters

Knowing God and Yourself

Andrew Petiprin

New
Growth
Press

WWW.NEWGROWTHPRESS.COM

New Growth Press, Greensboro, NC 27404
www.newgrowthpress.com
Copyright © 2018 by Andrew Petiprin

All rights reserved. No part of this publication may be reproduced, stored
in a retrieval system, or transmitted in any form by any means, electronic,
mechanical, photocopy, recording, or otherwise, without the prior
permission of the publisher, except as provided by USA copyright law.

Unless otherwise indicated, Scripture quotations are taken from *The Holy
Bible, English Standard Version.* Copyright © 2000; 2001 by Crossway
Bibles, a division of Good News Publishers. Used by permission. All rights
reserved.

Scripture verses marked NRSV are taken from the New Revised Standard
Version Bible, copyright © 1989 the Division of Christian Education of the
National Council of the Churches of Christ in the United States of America.
Used by permission. All rights reserved.

Scripture verses marked KJV are taken from the King James Version of the
Bible. Public domain.

Scripture verses marked BCP are taken from The Book of Common Prayer.
Public domain.

Cover Design: Faceout Books, faceoutstudio.com
Interior Typesetting and eBook: Lisa Parnell, lparnell.com

ISBN: 978-1-945270-93-2 (Print)
ISBN: 978-1-945270-94-9 (eBook)

Library of Congress Cataloging-in-Publication Data on file

Printed in the United States of America

25 24 23 22 21 20 19 18   1 2 3 4 5

CONTENTS

Acknowledgments   v

1. "I Believe in God"   1

2. The Main Character   9

3. The Impossible Union   28

4. The *Kerygma*   46

5. The Fire Within   65

6. Are You Being Saved?   84

7. Guaranteed Grace   101

8. The Life of the World to Come   121

9. Amen   142

   Endnotes   150

Acknowledgements

I am grateful first of all to my friend and colleague, Justin Holcomb, who encouraged me from my earliest thoughts about writing a book like this. His help at every step along the way has made this project possible. Special thanks to Kathryn Gillett for help in various essential ways, and especially for transcribing my sermons, parts of which have made their way into this book throughout. Mary Gillett was an enormous help too. I am deeply indebted to Steve Brown and everyone at Key Life. Christopher Wells and all of my colleagues at the Living Church are as good a cohort as anyone could wish for. My editor at New Growth Press, Barbara Juliani, has been a pleasure to work with. I am grateful also to Gretchen Logterman, and especially to Kenneth and Marjorie Cook, whose suggestions were most illuminating. Any and all deficiencies in this book are uniquely of my doing.

Many friends have been valuable collaborators over these years, and among them I especially single out Zachary Giuliano. Thanks to Ian Crafford for many edifying discussions, as well as for building my website. Matthew Turner not only continues to demonstrate truly Christian neighbor love, but proved particularly helpful to me in suggesting practical steps as the book neared production. Bishops Gregory Brewer and John Bauerschmidt have encouraged my writing as part of my ministry. David Peoples, Tim Nunez, Jonathan French, and the God Squad encourage me daily. My sisters, Mary Mullins and Karin Fields, read portions of the book in its early stages. Their love is indispensable. My mother's prayers have been the wind in my sails from the beginning.

God's greatest gift to me is my wife, Amber, and our children, Alexander and Aimee. I am thankful to them in more ways than I can count and I love them more than I can say.

Finally, this book originated in various teachings and sermons I offered to my former parishioners at St. Mary of the Angels in Orlando, Florida. Although I was their priest, they showed me what the truth of the gospel looked like and why it mattered. My gratitude to them knows no bounds.

1

"I Believe in God"

⟿

Everything changed in 2001. For those of us who remember that fateful day, the terrorist attacks of September 11 taught us that things were not what they seemed. We suddenly realized that four airplanes, two skyscrapers, a government building, and a patch of Pennsylvania farmland could be battlefields. For a brief period, many people—and especially people in the United States—felt a deep sense of disconnection from everything they had been raised to believe was secure. A few even dared to look into their own hearts and households to face a void that only something bigger than themselves, bigger than nations, and bigger than the world could explain. As the Anglican theologian Rowan Williams noted about his own experience in New York on the day the World Trade Center fell:

God always has to be rediscovered. Which means God always has to be heard or seen where there aren't yet words for him.[1]

When we face personal or national crises, we may find that the god we thought we were relying on (if we thought we were relying on a god at all), is a figment of our own imagination. Williams continues:

Perhaps it's when we try to make God useful in crises . . . that we take the first steps towards the great lie of religion: the god who fits our agenda.[2]

The crisis of the terrorist attacks of 2001 was looming in the background of my life when, after America's airports opened a few weeks later, I boarded a plane for London. I had won a scholarship to study at Oxford, and I moved abroad just at the moment when my own country seemed in unparalleled tumult. I was in tumult too. And the question before me was whether the god of my crises was, in fact, the true God. This crisis went all the way back to my childhood, to a deep, life-giving Christian worldview steeped in Bible stories, church choirs, youth groups, putting on the "whole armor of God" (Ephesians 6:10–18) every morning, and listening to my mother read the Chronicles of Narnia at bedtime. All of this had defined who I was, and for my young years it defined what I was doing in the world. But by the time I headed across the Atlantic as a twenty-one-year-old man, I had deep questions about whether any of it was real. Did I worship God, or the god who fit my agenda, and the agendas of my family and community?

I thought I knew better than everyone. This was especially true with religious leaders. If my pastor could not even be trusted to use proper grammar, how could he be trusted to teach me truth? I looked elsewhere for answers for a while. But the faith into which I was baptized as a baby and grew into as a child simply would not go away. But I needed a guarantee. How could I know that God's saving grace was active and real? And then I discovered poetry. Yes, poetry. Philosophy too. And painting, drama, and intellectual pursuits of all sorts. And I discovered that the vast majority of poems, paintings, plays, and other beautiful things throughout history had been done to the glory of God: Father, Son, and Holy Spirit. Christians could be sophisticated and creative because they knew the source of everything worth knowing and admiring. And they had to be humble, because the presence of the living God in their lives took them out of themselves. "Humble yourselves before the Lord," the Bible teaches us, "and he will exalt you" (James 4:10).

In that tumultuous fall of 2001, I was reading one poet in particular: T. S. Eliot. Eliot was an American who had emigrated to England. He was a brilliant young man who had studied at Harvard, Oxford, and the Sorbonne; and as he matured, he discovered that the only answer to the world's problems lay in the same answer that I, too, was beginning to discover. Eliot tried brilliantly to describe the chaos of a post–World War I world in his famous poem "The Waste Land." But there was no way to make sense of it. He came to find another answer—one that does not make false promises of a "war to end all wars," or innovations that claim to render the age-old afflictions powerless. What he found was the gospel of Jesus Christ, expressed in changeless doctrine that was designed to meet the needs of every age, and of every heart. This is what I was unconsciously looking for when I left for what turned out to be a three-year sojourn in England.

Eliot describes the cyclical quest for truth in his masterful series *The Four Quartets*. The world is full, Eliot tells us, of "hints and guesses, hints followed by guesses; and the rest is prayer, observance, discipline, thought, and action."[3] Like the journeys of Abraham and Moses, the psalmist, Paul, and Jesus himself, Eliot knew that everything meaningful points toward devotion to the one true and living God. He situates himself and his readers in a place of ceaseless exploration toward our Father, who makes our purpose clear: "You are here to kneel where prayer has been valid." This is the purpose of life: "to kneel where prayer has been valid." And to Eliot, prayer "is more than an order of words, the conscious occupation of the praying mind, or the sound of the voice praying."[4] Prayer is life. And so it makes all the difference in the world to know just who it is who first gives and then receives back the lives we live. Or to put it another way, to whom am I praying? Truth matters.

As it happened, I had almost no sooner touched down in England than I encountered a place where prayer had been valid for a long, long time. More than five hundred years before terrorists destroyed the World Trade Center and killed more than three thousand people, Christians were praying on the very spot where God had put me in order to rediscover him. I began attending the Holy Eucharist every morning and returning every evening to sit enraptured by a unique English prayer service called Choral Evensong. The place was

Magdalen College Chapel in Oxford, and as far as likely candidates go for places where prayer has been valid, this is as close to the top of the list as it comes. It also looms large in the story of another great twentieth-century Christian hero of mine, C. S. Lewis. Lewis was a contemporary of Eliot's and taught at Magdalen for many years. After his conversion to Christianity in the early 1930s, he prayed every day in the same sacred space where God had led me. I imagined him sitting in the stalls directly across from where I sat each night, only fifty years earlier. There in that historically and faithfully saturated environment, I took seriously for the first time what it meant to love God by loving the teachings he had delivered to Christians like Eliot and Lewis. And those teachings begin with this sentence:

> I believe in God, the Father almighty, creator of heaven and earth.

These are the first words of the formulation of the Christian faith that we now call the Apostles' Creed. The whole thing reads like this, and it is printed this way in my tradition:

> I believe in God, the Father almighty,
>   creator of heaven and earth.
> I believe in Jesus Christ, his only Son, our Lord.
>   He was conceived by the power of the Holy Spirit
>   and born of the Virgin Mary.
>   He suffered under Pontius Pilate,
>   was crucified, died, and was buried.
>   He descended to the dead.

On the third day he rose again.
He ascended into heaven,
and is seated at the right hand of the Father.
He will come again to judge the living and the dead.
I believe in the Holy Spirit,
the holy catholic Church,
the communion of saints,
the forgiveness of sins,
the resurrection of the body,
and the life everlasting. Amen.

The words are printed this way because they are meant to be recited aloud, alongside other people. Truth is not just for private intellectual assent, but public declaration. I said (in fact, I chanted) these words each night at Evensong alongside fellow worshipers when I was in the throes of my spiritual crisis, and I say them every day still. Sometimes the words roll out unconsciously. At other times I am bowled over by a particular line or two. The truth of God in Christ works this way. It is both a reliable workhorse and a derby winner.

From the earliest days of the Church, those baptized into the community professed the Apostles' Creed, and it remains in use today for the same purpose. And what do the words signify? To start, "I believe in God" means that I want more than myself. The "I" that I am sometimes proud of, sometimes ashamed of, and sometimes indifferent toward, wants to belong to the story of the great "I am." To say "I believe" acknowledges the way things are. I have a maker, and so do you. The world and everything in it once was not, and then was. The answer to the questions, "Who is God?" and "Who am I?" are therefore always intertwined. But this belief is not in a vague power. It is faith in a God who has revealed himself in specific ways, and principally in the Bible. Father, Son, and Holy Spirit are all there. The life of Christ is there. The Church is there. Forgiveness, resurrection, eternal life, and everything else is there. Most of all we learn, through all the stories of God's revelation to and interaction with our world, how the truth liberates us from our own illusions so that we may know God and ourselves. Jesus says, "If you abide in my word, you are truly my disciples, and you will know the truth, and the truth will set you free" (John 8:31–32).

This book champions truth, and asserts that the authentic teachings of the Christian faith are the best means of human flourishing. The Apostles' Creed is a useful lens through which we shall focus on a picture of this faith. In this picture will appear another creed, the Nicene Creed, along with various events in history when doctrine was debated and decided. Doctrine develops, but truth never changes. The purpose of doctrine is to make truth clearer than before, because our lives depend on it. In fact, it is my conviction that orthodox Christian belief is the only balm for our wounds in our inevitable times of distress like September 11; and it is also the joy of our hearts in times of blessing. It keeps us from thinking too highly of ourselves but also instills in us an infinite worth given by an all-loving God. It reminds us that there is a place to turn when we fall short.

Truth matters to me because I love God. I have tried and failed to get away from him. I have tried to avoid God and reject God, but I cannot escape his love. I invite you to explore this love with me. But a word of warning: the God of the Bible and the Church described by Christian doctrine does not fit my agenda, and he will not fit yours. By the end of this book, it is my hope that you will thank God that this is so. I myself am an Anglican, and indeed, an Episcopal priest. But this book is necessarily ecumenical. It is, after all, about transcendent truth enshrined in teachings that predate denominations. It is my hope that Roman Catholics and Eastern Orthodox Christians, as well as many Protestants, will be encouraged to examine their faith more closely—that they will rediscover the truth of God who puts denominational gods to shame. Finally, if this book says anything to seekers after truth with no background in Christianity (or indeed religion!), then I thank God from whom all blessings flow.

2

The Main Character

~

This is a book about God. And we assert from the start that "In him we live and move and have our being" (Acts 17:28). Only the true God can love us, and only the true God can receive our love in return. Only the true God can bear the weight of the hopes and expectations that we put on him. So who is he? What is his story? How is his truth relevant to us personally?

Traditionally, the centerpiece of Christian worship has been a service called the Great Vigil of Easter. It was done in the ancient Church and it is still done in many churches today. The congregation assembles as the sun is setting on the Saturday evening before Easter Sunday. The church is dark, and the first activity is lighting the "new fire," reminding us of the complete renewal of creation that begins in the resurrection of Jesus. The deacon chants "the light of Christ" and the building comes back to life after two days of tomb-like emptiness. The people hear the ancient hymn called the Exsultet, in which the Church reminds herself that "this is the night." Historically, this was also the most likely night for a new Christian to be baptized. And before any water was splashed or promises were made, the assembly sat in silence and listened to Bible stories. They soaked for a while in God's story in order to know their own stories. We need to soak in God's story now too.

We start with the very first story of all. "In the beginning, God created the heavens and the earth" (Genesis 1:1). The start of the Creed accords with the start of the Bible: "I believe in God, the Father Almighty, creator of heaven and earth." God is our Father who gives life to us, his children. We are created in his image and bear his likeness (Genesis 1:26). The first humans understood that their world was in perfect harmony with heaven. In this pristine moment at the dawn of life, there was no need to say "I believe," because existence was simply sharing the divine life. Adam and Eve had it all. Their Father loved them and they loved him. But being made in the image and likeness of God means being free—free even to choose our own misery; and so at this point our story takes an unnatural diversion from God's plot. Our ancestors in Eden set a precedent that torments us down to the present day—that we imagine God as a character in our story instead of living out our destiny as a character in his. For now, belief is before us as a choice: "I believe" or "I don't believe." Adam and Eve chose wrongly. They chose against truth. The image and likeness of God was marred and obscured in them and in us. But their choice wasn't the end of the story.

The truth matters, and belief in God's truth saves. As we follow some of the main characters in God's story, we learn how a story with a tragic twist gives way to a happy ending. The famous tale of Noah and the ark (Genesis 6:9–9:29) is our next stop. Here we encounter both the natural dead end of human freedom and the unexpected gift of a way out. Noah represents every person, and the ark prefigures the means of every person's hope of salvation. But Noah's story also raises a profoundly troubling concern. What kind of God would wipe most of the creatures he had made off the face of the earth? Put another way: If God is the main character, is he a good guy or a bad guy? If God is our Father, is he a good dad or an abusive maniac? This question tortures skeptics, and it even creeps into the unguarded minds of believers; but, in fact, it presupposes a false step. The god of this kind of question has never been the one in whom the Church has said in her creeds for more than two thousand years, "I believe." This god is not "The Father Almighty," but a jealous rival. He is either kindly or cruelly capricious—a vending-machine god who does what we expect when we offer him what he wants. This god, sadly, either does nothing or comes after us when we get it wrong. This is not the God who shows Noah the path to life, nor the God whose story we learn and affirm. This is not the true God at all.

The story of Noah's ark leads us into truth, and truth can often unsettle us before it comforts us. This story teaches us that we are capable of walking apart from God to such a degree that we might never find our way back. Indeed, like

Judas Iscariot who would have been better off not to have been born (Matthew 26:24), the people surrounding Noah and his family make God "sorry that he had made human-kind on the earth, and it grieved him to his heart" (Genesis 6:6 NRSV). Children's disobedience is often bad for them, and it is heartbreaking. We could even say that those who are lost in the flood are simply committing suicide. They choose over and over again to do the things that destroy them, and they bring down the whole world with them. Noah's neighbors are like someone who smokes or drinks excessively for decades and eventually succumbs to lung cancer or heart disease. In some cases, this sort of person often harms those around him too. Put this way, the big picture of this controversial thing called sin is writ large enough for all but the most hardened of hedonists to appreciate: Our actions have consequences, and not just for ourselves. God alone, the Father Almighty, can make things right.

Noah's obedience proves that even in the face of over-whelming opposition, we can choose to serve the God who made us. We can learn to see reality from God's perspective and act according to God's will. Moreover, we can see God for who he is. In the story of Noah, God doesn't stomp off in a huff, but remains with his people forever, grieving for their desire to make gods out of themselves. God takes what-ever little remnant of goodness he can find—in this case, one single family on earth—and uses it to transform everything else. He loves his creation and will save any part of it that wants to be saved.

But something else is at stake. The story of Noah's ark serves a specific purpose for Christians. Its meaning is picked up in no uncertain terms in the first book of Peter in the New Testament. Noah's salvation in the ark from the waters of the flood is a prefiguration of the saving work of God in Holy Baptism. Peter writes:

> Eight persons were brought safely through water. Baptism, which corresponds to this, now saves you, not as a removal of dirt from the body but as an appeal to God for a good conscience, through the resurrection of Jesus Christ. (1 Peter 3:20b–21)

All who come up from the sacramental waters climb aboard the vessel that we call the Church, a body born on the day of Pentecost but conceived many long centuries before in the couple Abraham and Sarah. And it is to them that we turn our attention now. In them, the story of God and us takes a decisive turn. The Father Almighty calls on Father Abraham and Mother Sarah.

Abraham becomes the figure in whom God works the specific plan to save the whole world—to save me and to save you. This claim may seem alarming. After all, Jesus is the one who saves. Jesus's coming is, as T. S. Eliot puts it, the "still point of the turning world."[1] But we must never forget that Jesus is the Messiah of Israel, and Israel begins with the calling of Abram (later Abraham), a man whose faithfulness was "reckoned . . . to him as righteousness" (Genesis 15:6 NRSV). His belief is illustrative for us. He does not just assent to intellectual propositions, but rather with his whole being he sees reality for what it is. Sarai (later Sarah), who is impossibly old to bear a child, laughs at first, as any of us would do; but she plays her part with faithfulness too, rejoicing in a God in whom nothing is impossible. The mission of Abraham and the many generations of his people to come—from great kings like David to a lowly peasant girl named Mary—was to be a light shining out from Israel to the whole world. Abraham chooses the truth. He believes. He lives in the light of who God is, and so can we.

Great struggles, however, stand in the way of the fulfillment of this promise, beginning with a most perplexing request God makes of Abraham. In the puzzling story from Genesis 22 known as the "binding of Isaac," Abraham is asked to sacrifice his son to the God who had finally come through on his promise. God chose Abraham and Sarah as the father and mother of a great multitude, and the next link in the chain is Isaac—no sooner born under astonishing circumstances than his life (and his line) are in mortal danger. Abraham's willingness to sacrifice his son reveals a seemingly insane faithfulness to God. In his faithfulness, Abraham knows God is in control. He tells Isaac, "God will provide for himself the lamb for a burnt offering, my son" (Genesis 22:8). God spares Isaac and provides a ram in Isaac's place, teaching us that he alone is capable of the full demonstration of sacrificial love required to change the story for mankind forever. Abraham's ram points to Jesus, the Lamb of God. The most famous verse in all of Scripture makes this clear:

> God so loved the world, that he gave his only Son, that whoever believes in him should not perish but have eternal life. (John 3:16)

There is no act of ours, however extreme, that can please God who needs nothing. God, not Abraham, will sacrifice his son. "I believe" means that I will reap the benefits of God's love.

God's story continues. The truth becomes clearer.

In Abraham's grandson, Jacob, God's holy nation gets its title. Jacob wrestles with a mysterious figure in a dream and, like his ancestor, receives a new name: Israel, which means "struggles with God" (Genesis 32:22–29). The moniker is appropriate for us too. In this fallen era, realizing our destiny to belong to God and do his will is always a challenge. Jacob's struggle tells us much about our own. And as we shall see, in Christ, the Church is Israel. Christians are spiritual heirs of everything promised to the first Jew and his entire lineage. So when we ask, "Who is God?" we find that God is the God of Abraham, Isaac, and Jacob—and also the God of the whole world. In you, God tells Abram, "all the families of the earth shall be blessed" (Genesis 12:3). Eventually his name is changed to Abraham, father of many nations (Genesis 17:5). God called Abram into truth and transformation, and God is calling you to the same.

But no sooner is Israel blessed with twelve sons (the fathers of the twelve tribes), than troubles in the family and on the land send God's people to Egypt. Joseph is sold into slavery by his jealous brothers—and, in a heart-wrenching turn of fate, finds himself able to save his people, who are starving and suffering from drought (Genesis 37–50). Joseph is a top official serving the pharaoh, and Joseph's family is therefore welcome with open arms. But eventually "there arose a new king over Egypt, who did not know Joseph" (Exodus 1:8). God then acts yet again—this time through the Exodus

(Exodus 14), the archetypal narrative for what God does for and through all his people, including you and me. This story contains the essence of what God gives: freedom—freedom from earthly slave masters, freedom from fear, freedom from the powers of darkness, freedom from our own terrible choices, freedom from our pain, freedom from the false selves that we construct. Like all the best stories, hearing this one repeatedly makes it both richer and simpler: God is the One who saves, and we are the ones who need saving.

The Old Testament rolls on from there, with one story after another of rise and fall, success and screwup, dependence on God and rejection of God. Judges come and go. Kings come and go. Prophets plead with God's people (and with us) to return to the path of life. In the prophecies of Isaiah, Ezekiel, and in the glorious vision of the gathering of God's people in the book of the prophet Zephaniah,[2] we are given a foretaste of how this saving was meant to happen from the beginning, and who this God is who is doing it.

Then at long last comes the Messiah—the one hinted at, guessed, and hoped for—the great king of David's line who will finally bring God's reign to bear on earth. Much to Israel's surprise, however, this king is born in the most ignoble of circumstances, many miles from his family's backwater home. Luke describes the familiar scene in a stark, intimate way:

> [Mary] gave birth to her firstborn son and wrapped him in swaddling cloths and laid him in a manger, because there was no place for them in the inn. (Luke 2:7)

The angels announce his birth, and the lowly shepherds praise the king whose reign will unfold most unexpectedly. For one thing, the Messiah was not expected to die, let alone by means of the imperial power's most shameful device, the cross. And then Jesus did what no one had ever done before. He defeated death itself[3] and rose again, shining in majesty, three days later. He appeared to his disciples and ascended to our Father in heaven. These elements are well known to most people as the very essence of the story of Jesus, the Son of God—born of a virgin, crucified, raised, and glorified. Only in hindsight does the person and activity of Jesus fit the arc of the story perfectly. His coming was the centerpiece of the grand design for God and his dealings with us all along; and in the aftermath of Jesus's ascension to the Father, the Church found herself needing a grammar to put the pieces of the puzzle together forever. Out of this need, Christian doctrine was born. And here the story of the Father Almighty becomes the story of the Holy Trinity.

GOD'S DOCTRINE

Many people throughout history lived in ignorance of the name and stories of the one true and living God. Some still do, but everyone may call upon him. In fact, all people are always looking for him. All the people of the earth are sons and daughters of Adam and Eve, called to be sons and daughters of God. Whatever strivings human beings have made, whatever stirrings they have felt in their hearts, whatever idols they have erected to fulfill their natural urge to worship, the

God of "In the beginning"—who raised up one holy people, Israel, and now is professed in the Christian creeds—has been the ground of it all. Every glimmer of truth expressed in pagan myths, every feeling of otherworldly presence, and every good and holy thing done by one person for another have come to find their ultimate meaning in the opening words of the Apostles' Creed: "I believe in God, the Father almighty, creator of heaven and earth."

But the Father isn't alone. God is three and God is one. The sacred declaration of ancient Israel remains as true as ever: "Hear, O Israel, the LORD our God, the LORD is one" (Deuteronomy 6:4). Equally true are the words of John the Evangelist: "In the beginning was the Word, and the Word was with God, and the Word was God" (John 1:1). Likewise the words on the lips of Jesus himself: "The Father and I are one" (John 10:30 NRSV). And then there is the Holy Spirit, operating in perfect unity with the Father and the Son from all eternity. The Spirit is no mere "agent" of God (for that is called an "angel"), but rather God's direct presence in his creation—a presence that the Bible makes abundantly clear. This unity is called the Holy Trinity, and it is no invention of overactive minds. The Trinity is the eternal nature and being of God, as demonstrated by the first story:

> In the beginning, God created the heavens and the earth. The earth was without form and void, and darkness was over the face of the deep. And the Spirit of God was hovering over the face of the waters. And God said, "Let there be light," and there was light. (Genesis 1:1–3)

The God that Jesus calls Father creates through his Word (whom John tells us is Jesus) and with the power of his Spirit (the same word in both Hebrew and Greek for "wind"). The Holy Trinity jumps out from the very first verses of Scripture.

In the early Church, various aspirants to the Christian faith stumbled over the idea of the Trinity. Some stumble over it now. There have always been people who, in an effort to understand for themselves the mysteries of faith, have misconstrued the nature of God. Such people were and are called "heretics"—those who choose a view of God that darkens rather than illuminates. Heretics—both very simply and very elaborately—mistake God for something he is not. A heresy that demands our attention now is Arianism, which created a need for a more robust creed than the Apostles' Creed. The result was the Nicene Creed, still professed by most Christians today:

> We believe in one God,
>> the Father, the Almighty.
>> maker of heaven and earth,
>> of all that is, seen and unseen.
> We believe in one Lord, Jesus Christ,
>> the only Son of God,
>> eternally begotten of the Father,
>> God from God, Light from Light,
>> true God from true God,
>> begotten, not made,
>> of one Being with the Father.
>> Through him all things were made.
>> For us and for our salvation

he came down from heaven:
by the power of the Holy Spirit
he became incarnate from the Virgin Mary,
and was made man.
For our sake he was crucified under Pontius Pilate;
he suffered death and was buried.
On the third day he rose again
in accordance with the Scriptures;
he ascended into heaven
and is seated at the right hand of the Father.
He will come again in glory to judge the living and
the dead,
and his kingdom will have no end.
We believe in the Holy Spirit, the Lord, the giver of life,
who proceeds from the Father and the Son.
With the Father and the Son he is worshiped and
glorified.
He has spoken through the Prophets.
We believe in one holy catholic and apostolic Church.
We acknowledge one baptism for the forgiveness of
sins.
We look for the resurrection of the dead,
and the life of the world to come. Amen.

Now we wonder: how did we get this creed, and why do
we need it?

To answer this question, we turn to an ancient heretic
named Arius (d. 336). Arius was an extremely public-relations-
savvy priest, who asserted that on the most fundamental level
attested by Scripture, Jesus is a creature and not God. To Arius,

the Apostles' Creed's "I believe in God, the Father Almighty" did not acknowledge the divinity of Jesus. In fact, it forbade it. Arius's heresy is sometimes classified as "subordinationism," and at first glance seems an acceptable underpinning to a statement like "I believe in God, the Father almighty." If the Father is God, then how can the Son or the Holy Spirit also be God? If the Father is almighty, how can the Son or the Holy Spirit be almighty as well? To Arius and his followers, any idea that the Father shares the fullness of the divine life with the Son and the Holy Spirit is absurd. "There once was a time when the Son was not,"[4] Arius and his camp reportedly declared—the first of what we might now call "bumper-sticker" theologies.

Arius's opponents, meanwhile, maintained that he was essentially expressing belief in one God and two creatures—utter blasphemy. The response to Arius was a passion for truth, resulting in the Nicene Creed, crafted to establish the parameters for what a Christian means when he or she declares "I believe in God."

The formation of the Nicene Creed is a major turning point in world history, and it has everything to do with interpreting the story of God and his people. Arian heretics were reading the Bible one way, and their opponents (whom we now call "orthodox") were reading it another way. Here we face the inevitable: Scripture must be interpreted, and decisions must be made about it. To declare "I believe in God" does not, in the end, allow for my God and your God—or indeed, for the notion that we all have it wrong and the real God is something else entirely. If there is one thing that the Old Testament tells us about God, it is that he is active in history and reveals himself to his people. The violent debates (and violent is the right word) between parties in the early fourth century AD over what would come to be called the Holy Trinity is far from the product of ignorance or arrogance (although, of course, one or two people who held right beliefs may have been ignorant, arrogant, or both!). The conclusion they fought about mattered for the Church then, and it matters for the Church now. A heretic is not one who simply disagrees with other Christians about a particular moral issue or favors one set of theological imagery over another. A heretic is one who bows down to an idol. The god of the heretic is not the God of the Bible and the Church.

It is difficult, and for our purposes unnecessary, to reconstruct exactly what happened at the Council of Nicaea, but it is safe to say that the first Christian Roman Emperor, Constantine, wanted order for the Church. It simply would not do to have different camps claiming to possess the authentic faith any more than it would do for God to leave the sea and sky mixed up when he created the earth. Constantine summoned the bishops in the year AD 325 at Nicaea in modern-day Turkey, near the imperial court at the new capital of the empire, the eponymous Constantinople. The bishops were tasked not only with working out how the Father related to the Son and the Holy Spirit, but also to decide on how to keep Easter, to create church laws, and to reform church structures.

At Nicaea, the great champions of the Trinity were Bishop Alexander of Alexandria and, more importantly, his assistant Athanasius (ca. 296–376). The highly contentious but ultimately beautifully defensible formula that won the day and eventually vanquished Arianism depended on one

Greek word, *homoousios*, "of one being" or "of one essence." Although this word is not found in the Bible, the concept behind it is deeply biblical. It takes deadly seriously Jesus's words of unity with his Father, extrapolating logically that if the Father was eternal and nothing pertaining to an eternal being could ever come to be, then it stood to reason that the Father was indeed eternally a Father. The image of light and its source became a crucial descriptive tool included in the creed as well: "God from God, light from light." A star is not a star without the light that it emits. The star's light is both one and the same as the star and yet somehow different—but different not because of essence, activity, or chronology, but rather by virtue of coming from a source, purely and simply. Light, then, is always begotten of its source and of the same stuff. Likewise, the source is never without that which it begets. In this way the Son is eternally begotten of the Father. In like manner, the Church chose—with an eye to biblical precision—to say of the Spirit that he "proceeds" from the Father (John 15:26), being coeternal with the Father and the Son. And there you have the truth: Father, Son, and Holy Spirit. God.

After the Council of Nicaea, just as before it, God's revelation of himself as Trinity was known and yet had to be taught and inculcated into the piety of the people. None of the bishops present at Nicaea walked away thinking they had done anything other than correct a particular heresy. Likewise, they did not imagine they had established a teaching that would never be questioned. There was work to be done as Christianity spread and grew. For us who have inherited faith in the God of Israel, such work is to be expected. Our forefathers the Jews were commanded to recite the aforementioned

shema ("Hear, O Israel . . .") as often as possible, along with
the Ten Commandments:

> Bind them as a sign on your hand, fix them as an emblem
> on your forehead, and write them on the doorposts of
> your house and on your gates. (Deuteronomy 6:8–9 NRSV)

As we shall explore in chapter 4, we must learn, relearn, and
remember who the God is who has called us into communion with him. For Christians, this means getting things
straight about the Holy Trinity, not so that all the faithful
can win intellectual arguments but so that they could "worship in spirit and truth" (John 4:24). For nearly sixty years
after Nicaea, the Church's finest minds set themselves to this
task, and none were greater in the Greek-speaking tradition
than the so-called Cappadocian fathers (ca. 350–400): the
brothers Basil of Caesarea and Gregory of Nyssa, and their
good friend Gregory Nazianzen (called "the Theologian").
Gregory Nazianzen, in particular, took the teachings of the
great Origen of Alexandria (ca. 185–254) and of others in the
tradition of theologians in Antioch and Constantinople, and
articulated the faith afresh as the Church moved forward
from Nicaea. Among Gregory's many writings, the most
precious are his *Five Theological Orations*, which inspire the
Christian heart to see only a God who could create, save, and
sustain as Father, Son, and Holy Spirit; and this is the God to
whom Christians pray, sing hymns, and offer incense. This
is the God in whom Christians place their ultimate hope. In
the Latin tradition, Augustine of Hippo (354–430) stakes the

same claim. Gregory, Augustine, and all true theologians make the faith of the Church perfectly sensible.

The Trinity is not three parts of God nor three versions of God, but a single God subsisting in three persons (in Greek, *hypostases*), united in essence and operation. The Holy Trinity summoned a wandering herdsman named Abram and set aside one nation to be the means of salvation for all the others. The Holy Trinity chose Moses to deliver his people from slavery in Egypt, and invited him to the top of a mountain to learn what God wanted for them. The Holy Trinity sustained the faithful remnant of Israel when they were run out of their land by conquering empires. It was the Holy Trinity that the world came to know in the person of Jesus Christ. It is the Holy Trinity that the Church on earth and in heaven worships and adores now and for all ages. It is the Holy Trinity in whom Christians say, "I believe." It is the Holy Trinity who loves you.

MY STORY

Who, then, am I in relation to God the Holy Trinity? The order of things matters greatly as we ask questions like this one. God is prior to me and prior to everything else that is and has ever been. God has no maker, and I do. My existence depends completely on his. Therefore, theology always precedes anthropology. We cannot start with ourselves and get to God, but rather we must start with God to arrive at our own identity. Conversion stories usually prove this rule. When a person is won over to God, it often feels like self-discovery in the place where God has already set up shop. St. Paul tells the Corinthians that a person who turns to Christ is one whose "veil is removed" (2 Corinthians 3:16). St. Augustine says about his own conversion experience:

> Late have I loved you, beauty so old and so new: late have I loved you. And see, you were within and I was in the external world and sought you there. . . . You were with me, and I was not with you. (Confessions X. xxvii.38)

To become someone who is able to say "I believe in God" is to take one's place in the cosmic narrative of God, who is love. The believer is one whose Father is in heaven, whose joys and sorrows are mapped onto God incarnate, Jesus Christ, and whose life is animated by God the Holy Spirit. A Christian is naturally biblical and trinitarian in his or her bones.

A Christian self is also selfless. To say "I believe in God" is to concede that living as if "I believe in me" is a pathetic fallacy. To believe in God is to understand myself as infinitely worthy, lovable, and capable; and also not the One who judges me thus. Utter dependence upon God, however, does not mean that my destiny is to melt away into a divine soup—for my "self," to disappear. It is precisely the opposite. Salvation is not annihilation, but transformation. John writes, "Beloved, we are God's children now, and what we will be has not yet appeared; but we know that when he appears we shall be like him, because we shall see him as he is. And everyone who thus hopes in him purifies himself as he is pure" (1 John 3:2–3).

To believe in God is to understand my story as a beautiful part of his story, which ends for me by being truly like him, purified as he is pure. The broken "I" that is offered eternal life will become the radiant "I" that properly belongs there— like Adam and Eve before it all went wrong. And the "I" that worships the true and living God on this side of eternity is the one who longs in his deepest heart to be refashioned alongside the rest of the created order. Here the whole notion of "I" becomes gloriously muddled. The God into whose fellowship I am baptized is the One who called me to that moment of initiation. God, in other words, is the one doing all of the work, all of the time.

The goal, then, of a human life is cooperation with the Holy Trinity and participation now in what will one day be reality. It is my job to be a son or a daughter to my Father in heaven. As at the Great Vigil of Easter, a human life is a soaking in the story of God, coming to realize that it is the story of me. God's story teaches me that the way I am ordered matters to him who made me. I have been made and must be remade. If I imagine myself the main character, I will not triumph as a hero, nor even die a brave martyr. I will be utterly forgotten. In God's story, however, I ride all the way to glory. The second person of the Trinity, Jesus Christ, is the pathway to this destination; and it is specifically to him that we must now turn our attention.

3

The Impossible Union

❧

Who is Jesus Christ? This is the most important question ever asked. I invite you to explore its answer with me. Jesus takes up the biggest part of the Apostles' and Nicene Creeds. Getting Jesus right puts the rest of Christian truth in place. Getting Jesus right also puts a person's life in place. How is it that God is three *and* one? How is it that God is infinitely "other" and yet completely intimate? How do I love my neighbor as myself? These questions depend on what we make of Jesus Christ. In fact, as you may have noticed, the controversy over the orthodox doctrine of God expressed in the Nicene Creed (that is, the Holy Trinity) had everything to do with Jesus. Arius concluded that Jesus was not God. Christians say that he is. But he is also a human being. How confusing. Why should anyone care?

In the Gospels of Matthew, Mark, Luke, and John, Jesus performs miracles and speaks with divine authority. He is resurrected. He loves in ways that seem impossibly difficult. But Jesus is also just like us. He may have been begotten of the Father before all worlds, but he was also born of Mary. He ate food, faced temptation, yet without sin (Hebrews 4:14–16), and "increased in wisdom and in stature" (Luke 2:52). He had a human family, lived under the yoke of imperial government, and kept the traditions of his people. He suffered and died. He is "the way, and the truth, and the life" (John 14:6).

Jesus was both fully God and fully man. He was neither one appearing as the other nor a hybrid of the two, but a mysterious single subject that bridges the gap between two realities—God's and ours. T. S. Eliot describes it like this:

> The hint half guessed, the gift half understood, is Incarnation. Here the impossible union.[1]

Scripturally derived doctrine makes this impossible union crystal clear. The truth matters, and it is accessible to us.

THE STORY OF THE MESSIAH

Jesus was a common name among the people of Israel. In fact, one of the greatest heroes in the story of God and his people bore this name, translated in this earlier instance as "Joshua." Joshua, not Moses, was the one who led God's people across the Jordan River to the earthly realm that had been allotted to them by Yahweh (Joshua 3–4). Joshua fought in front of his compatriots (Joshua 6–10) and carried on the work of leadership begun in the first Jew, Abraham. Many hundreds of years later, in a remote part of the northern edge of the once-united kingdom of Israel and Judah, a much greater leader than Joshua, a much greater prophet than Moses, and a much more obedient listener than Adam came into the world. In fact, with Jesus's coming, the stories of all these other memorable human beings came to fruition, along with the stories of David, Solomon, Ruth, Esther, Job, Isaiah, Jeremiah, and Daniel, just to name a few. Jesus took over their stories and perfected them. In Jesus, the stories of everyone who came before took on new meaning, and the stories of all who would come after have a common climax. As the Messiah of Israel, Jesus is what Irenaeus of Lyons (d. ca. 195) called the "recapitulation" of all of the heroes and stories of God's people as recorded in the Bible. Everything that came before Jesus pointed toward him. He is the holy reality that overtakes the holy imitations—the prototype of which everyone and everything else had been a copy (with varying degrees of likeness). We may even say that Jesus is the human being, the son of man, the last Adam (1 Corinthians 15:45). Humanity is measured against him.

Jesus is also the Jew. As noted in the last chapter in the calling of Abraham, God raised up one people, the Jews, as the means through which he would save the whole world and restore what had fallen in Adam and Eve. Jesus, as the Messiah, is the Savior of all; but his universal identity and work can sometimes obscure the particular quality of who exactly he is and what he did. That is, we will misunderstand how he came to redeem the whole world if we do not properly understand how he is first the redeemer of one group of people of whom he is the foremost representative. Jesus fixed the universal problem of Adam's disobedience by perfecting the particular instance of Abraham's obedience. In sum, he saves the world because he came to save his people.

By the time of Jesus's birth, Israel had definite and sometimes competing expectations of what the Messiah would be. At every turn, Jesus fulfilled these hopes by turning them upside down. Jesus is the anointed one ("Christos")—a prophet and a king. His lineage is indeed kingly and he is born in Bethlehem, David's royal city; but he is delivered in a barn and laid in an animal trough. Lowly shepherds and wandering foreign astrologers—not the ruling elite—bow down to him and honor him. All four Gospel accounts tell us that he enters Jerusalem not on a war horse, but on a donkey (Matthew 21:1–9; Mark 11:1–10; Luke 19:28–40; John 12:12–19). He preaches not of the great city's glory, but of its demise (Luke 19:41–44). His vision of restoring Israel is not one of ethnic pride, but of revealing the ever-present kingdom in the midst of us all. He comes to rule heaven and earth as king—paradoxically both the heir and the father, both successor and master of King David.[2] He is crowned not with gold and jewels, but with well-wrought thorns. He defeated Israel's enemies not by leading armies into battle but by walking away in triumph from the empty tomb.

As we shall explore further in the next chapter, Jesus's coming did not trigger an automatic salvation effect; rather, he saved by fulfilling a large number of obligations described in the Old Testament, culminating in his death and resurrection. Thus, even as John the Evangelist declares "the Word became flesh and dwelt among us" (John 1:14), in the same chapter John the Baptist adds, "Behold, the Lamb of God"

(John 1:29). The incarnation was the first step of the Messiah's saving mission on earth. The "impossible union" is the beginning of impossible activity. God became man so that he could die for our sins, and defeat death and the devil once and for all. The glory of the incarnation is a seed that comes to fruition in the resurrection.

Everything, however, depends on exactly who it was who came into the world and did what he did. Was Jesus a godlike man or a manlike God? Here we must return to the development of doctrine. As we shall see, salvation rests on the fact that he was neither God simply appearing as a man nor a man whose human soul had simply been displaced by a divine soul, but rather fully God and fully man. He did not seem like one while actually being the other. He was the God-man—one person uniting but never mixing the human and the divine. Pope Leo the Great (ca. 400–461) puts it this way:

> While the distinctness of both natures and substances is preserved, and both meet in one Person, lowliness is assumed by majesty, weakness by power, mortality by eternity; and in order to pay the debt of our condition, the inviolable nature has been united to the passible, so that, as the appropriate remedy for our ills, one and the same "Mediator between God and men, the man Christ Jesus," might from one element be capable of dying, and from the other be incapable.[3]

Jesus had to have one foot firmly in each camp in order to bridge the gap between the two. Jesus called himself the "Son of Man"—a title from Daniel's vision, in which the son of man "was given dominion and glory and a kingdom" (Daniel 7:14). In Jesus, everything pertaining to God and everything pertaining to human beings are at long last in perfect accord. The study of how this is so is called Christology, and there is no theological discipline that has more at stake.

THE GOD-BEARER

Both the Apostles' and Nicene Creeds have more to say about Jesus than about the other two persons of the Trinity, and they vary subtly from each other. Here we compare side-by-side what each creed says specifically about Jesus:

Apostles' Creed	Nicene Creed
I believe in Jesus Christ, his only Son, our Lord. He was conceived by the power of the Holy Spirit and born of the Virgin Mary. He suffered under Pontius Pilate, was crucified, died, and was buried. He descended to the dead. On the third day he rose again. He ascended into heaven, and is seated at the right hand of the Father. He will come again to judge the living and the dead.	We believe in one Lord, Jesus Christ, the only Son of God, eternally begotten of the Father, God from God, Light from Light, true God from true God, begotten, not made, of one Being with the Father. Through him all things were made. For us and for our salvation he came down from heaven: by the power of the Holy Spirit he became incarnate from the Virgin Mary, and was made man. For our sake he was crucified under Pontius Pilate; he suffered death and was buried. On the third day he rose again in accordance with the Scriptures; he ascended into heaven and is seated at the right hand of the Father. He will come again in glory to judge the living and the dead, and his kingdom will have no end.

Both creeds tell the story of Jesus; but the Nicene Creed fleshes out biblical truths that prevent our falling into error. In general, the elaborations in the Nicene Creed not found in the Apostles' Creed make the case for how God, the transcendent ground of all being, became a feeble creature like you and me. But many who accepted the Nicene Creed did not see things this way, and it would take the better part of a century to arrive at the definition that addresses the "impossible union." This is the story that culminates in the Council of Chalcedon (451). In this story we see how doctrine develops, but truth never changes.

As you may have noticed, the creeds contain two proper names: Mary and Pontius Pilate. The role that each of these two figures plays in the biblical accounts of the life of Christ have a profound effect on our understanding who Jesus was and is. We shall return to Pilate later, but Mary demands our attention now. Mary's story has rightly inspired generations. She believed in Jesus when he was still growing within her. She knew her Savior more intimately than any other. Mary's "yes" to God is the most profound example of human service to him in the entire Bible. Mary, although a creature like you and me, did what you and I may find impossible. "My soul magnifies the Lord," she sings in Luke 1:46, and she reveals a fullness of grace that we are quite right to bring to mind as often as we can. Mary points us to Jesus over and over again. But what exactly did Mary do by giving birth to Jesus? And what should we call her? These are the questions that proved to be the catalyst for major controversies about how we understand the Jesus we profess our faith in.

In the same tumultuous fourth century that produced the Nicene Creed, Christians in various places (particularly those in modern-day Syria and Turkey) began questioning the use of the Greek term *theotokos*. Mary was often called this in worship in Egypt and elsewhere, and it means "God-bearer" or "Mother of God." Here again, as we saw with the word *homoousios* in the Nicene Creed, we find in *theotokos* a non-biblical word that becomes rightly enshrined in Christian doctrine. Jesus is by nature God's son and not Joseph's. The angel Gabriel tells Mary: "The Holy Spirit will come upon you, and the power of the Most High will overshadow you; therefore the child to be born will be holy; he will be called Son of God" (Luke 1:35 NRSV). We cannot call God's Son something other than God. Nowhere is this more apparent than in the nine "I am" statements of John's Gospel (John 6:35; 8:12; 10:9, 11, 14; 11:25; 14:6; 15:1, 5). Once again we turn to Pope Leo the Great, whose "Tome" would clarify Christian doctrine forever:

> To hunger, thirst, to be weary, and to sleep is evidently human. But to feed five thousand men with five loaves, and to bestow on the woman of Samaria that living water, to drink of which can secure one from thirsting again; to walk on the surface of the sea with feet that sink not, and by rebuking the storm to bring down the "uplifted waves," is unquestionably divine.[4]

We must assign to one nature of Jesus (the human one) all things that we experience and God does not. We must assign to another nature (the divine one) all things that Jesus is recorded to have done in Scripture that are possible only for God.

To those who favored the term *theotokos*, Mary truly bore
God (and a man). And to say that she did not bear God is to
say that Jesus is not God. This denial takes us right back to
Arianism and the controversies that created a need for the
Nicene Creed and the doctrine of the Holy Trinity. Some
Christians, however, argued otherwise. There are many memorable personalities and intricate arguments over the course
of many years, but for our purposes the debate between Cyril
of Alexandria (d. 444) and Nestorius of Constantinople (d.
ca. 451) is the most illustrative.

Nestorius taught that Jesus was a special man anointed as
God's Messiah and was obedient to God's commands even
unto death. Nestorius's Mary, therefore, did not give birth to
God. Nestorius believed that divinity negates the possibility
of birth, and so to him, Mary simply gave birth to a human
male, Jesus of Nazareth. Nestorius said in one letter that if
Mary bore God she would be giving birth to one older than
herself, which is absurd.[5] Nestorius's Christ was not God,
leaving us to ask ourselves how any man, however good,
could possibly save the whole of humanity and all creation.

The Bible leaves no room for any version of Nestorianism,
and Cyril of Alexandria said so. Cyril concluded that the only
way to avoid Nestorius's logical dead end was to keep Mary
on the pedestal she was already on. She was the *theotokos*,
the God-bearer. If Jesus was not God in Mary's womb, then
he had no chance of saving us from our sins (Matthew 1:21)
and was unworthy of the wise men's worship (Matthew 2:11).
If God was not brought up by Joseph, presented in the temple
(Luke 2:22), taken on a yearly pilgrimage to Jerusalem (Luke
2:41), and "increased in wisdom and stature" (Luke 2:52),

then he neither hung on the cross nor defeated the grave. No mere man's birth, death, or even resurrection could do anything for any other man or woman. Jesus had to be God, and God is always God. In Cyril's words: "When they say that the Word of God did not become flesh, or rather did not undergo birth from a woman according to the flesh, they bankrupt the economy of salvation."[6]

The matter of Jesus's two natures united in one person came to the fore during several messy attempts to bring the Church together in councils in the early 400s. In 431, at the Council of Ephesus, *theotokos* was definitively accepted as the right way to refer to Mary. The council decreed:

> If anyone will not confess that the Emmanuel is very God, and that therefore the Holy Virgin is the Mother of God (*theotokos*), inasmuch as in the flesh she bore the Word of God made flesh (as it is written, "The Word was made flesh"): let him be anathema.[7]

The "him" here starts with Nestorius, and "anathema" means cast out of the communion of the Church. Cyril's position had won the day; but the more delicate question of how to express the union of God and man in Jesus was left unresolved for the next twenty years. Disagreements at later church councils resulted in one party condemning the other and claiming foul play. Many attempts at formulas of union were drafted and discarded. Confusion reigned amid anathemas and schisms, until the fourth and largest of all the ecumenical councils was convened in Chalcedon, near Constantinople, in the year 451. Cyril's work was crucial in what

became the Chalcedonian Decree (still adhered to by most
Christians on earth), but Pope Leo the Great's Tome insisted
on the "two natures" language to resolve disputes about
Christ's identity. Thanks to Cyril and Leo, Christians finally
had a grammar for understanding how the world is healed
by the Incarnation of Christ. The formula explicitly reaffirms
Nicaea (325) and the decision about Mary's title (431), and
declares Jesus to be

> in two natures without confusion, without change, with-
> out division, without separation—the difference of the
> natures being by no means taken away because of the
> union, but rather the distinctive character of each nature
> being preserved, and [each] combining in one Person.[8]

The Council of Chalcedon opened up many cans of worms
that still create ecumenical problems and was overly influ-
enced by imperial political agendas, but the main thrust of the
Chalcedonian Decree would be of the greatest importance to
Christians down to the present day. One person: Jesus. Two
natures: fully human and fully divine. From the moment of
his conception in Mary's womb right to the present moment
as he reigns in glory at the right hand of the Father, Jesus was
and is both God and a man. That's the truth.

Many other Christological controversies followed in the
years after Chalcedon. If Jesus is God and man, does he have
both a human mind and a divine mind? The answer proved
to be "yes." Does Jesus have a divine and human will? Again,
yes. Every imaginable thing that pertains to God was and
is present in Jesus Christ. Likewise, no part of the human

experience was and is lacking either. For Christians today, all of these decisions may be summed up by the words of Gregory Nazianzen, whose work foreshadowed Cyril's: "That which he has not assumed he has not healed; but that which is united to his Godhead is also saved."[9] Jesus's death on the cross wipes away our sins and his resurrection offers us eternal life, because only God, united to a perfect human, could rewrite the ending of the story of Adam and Eve. Only the God-man's sacrifice fulfills what Abraham's near offering of Isaac only hinted at. Only the God-man who both gives and obeys the Law could perfect what Moses taught in the wilderness. Only in God's feeling every twinge of human anguish could we ever hope to live without it.

WHAT IS TRUTH?

In perhaps the most famous passage from Fyodor Dostoevsky's masterpiece *The Brothers Karamazov* called "The Grand Inquisitor," a tale is told by Ivan Karamazov, the atheist brother of Alyosha, a novice monk, with whom he is engaged in a deep theological struggle. Ivan proposes a scenario in which Jesus returns to earth at the height of the Spanish Inquisition in the seventeenth century. This is not his final coming in glorious majesty to judge the living and the dead, but an inexplicable reappearance. As with his first visit, Jesus creates a buzz. He has a magnetic presence. Dostoevsky writes:

> The people are irresistibly drawn to Him, they surround Him, they flock about Him, follow Him. He moves silently

in their midst with a gentle smile of infinite compassion. The sun of love burns in His heart, light and power shine from His eyes, and their radiance, shed on the people stirs their hearts with responsive love. He holds out His hands to them, blesses them, and a healing virtue comes from contact with Him, even with His garments.[10]

The people know the real thing when they see it.

Jesus continues to replicate some of the miracles he performed during his original stay, but before he knows it (like the first time around) he is hauled in to face the authorities, with the irony being that the authorities he faces are successors of the very ones he left on earth as his body and commissioned to evangelize the whole world more than 1,500 years earlier. The Church to which he has given the power to bind and loose (Matthew 16:19) now believes herself to have this power even over the One who granted it. The Grand Inquisitor, a cardinal in the Roman Catholic Church, is a hardened cynic—a long, long way from Mary Magdalene's wondrous utterance, "I have seen the Lord" (John 20:18). When we meet this fellow, we feel pretty far from mystical revelry as well. "You promised them the bread of Heaven," the Grand Inquisitor tells Jesus, "but . . . can it compare with earthly bread in the eyes of the weak, ever sinful and ignoble race of man?"[11] He concludes: "You did yourself lay the foundation for the destruction of your kingdom, and no one is more to blame for it."[12]

The Grand Inquisitor reminds us of the infamous inclusion of Pontius Pilate in the Christian creeds. He is the one so befuddled by the king, prophet, and priest standing before him that his only conclusion is an eerily timeless question,

"What is truth?" The words of Jesus certainly answer this question ("I am the way, the truth, and the life"), but more importantly, the big picture that we have been looking at in this chapter consigns this query to the top of an enormous pile of skeptical jargon. If the story of Jesus is true, then Pilate's paralysis is truly tragic. The world has Pilate's choice always before it and stands at the crossroad of glory and misery. Pilate rejected the "impossible union" long before Nestorius did. And yet, even Pilate had his doubts about rejecting the truth. When the chief priests ask him not to write "King of the Jews," but rather "This man said I am king of the Jews" above Jesus on the cross, Pilate replies, "What I have written I have written" (John 19:22). How many agnostics and atheists in our own day almost stumble into truth like Pilate? Perhaps you find yourself conflicted in this way.

PERSONAL RELATIONSHIP

God is relational. He is nearer to us than we are to ourselves and more loving than any human relation could ever be to us. And in the depth of our hearts, we must decide to belong to him. We must either choose the side of Mary or Pilate. Truth or an imitation. A savior or an imposter.

Jesus's interactions with others in the Bible make it clear that he, like his Father, desires to be in relationship with us; and the key to understanding this relationship is remembering that God always initiates it. When I asked Jesus to be in my life when I was a small boy, it was really an acknowledgment that he was already there. In John's Gospel the future apostle Nathanael is called by the apostle Philip to "Come and see" Jesus (John 1:46). But before Nathanael arrives, Jesus has already seen him and figured him out. Nathanael asks, "How do you know me?" (John 1:48), thinking that he was the one who was coming to meet Jesus, when in fact Jesus had "met" Nathanael before he had even arrived. Authentic biblical interpretation and the development of Christian doctrine work the same way. When we come to an authentic conclusion, we realize that God has been the one showing us the way all along. Our coming to Jesus is simply our reminder that Jesus has already come to us.

As any human being would be, Jesus is interested in who people think he is. "Some say John the Baptist, but others Elijah, and still others Jeremiah or one of the prophets," Peter says to Jesus (Matthew 16:14). But Jesus wants to know what Peter thinks—and he wants to know what you think. "You are the Messiah, the Son of the living God," Peter declares (Matthew 16:16). Deciding who Jesus is to you matters enormously in accepting his offer to relate to you. Peter, of course, will come to deny Jesus three times; but he will make up for his betrayal with three "I love you's" (John 21:15–19). Jesus allows Peter a triplicate restoration, and he is always willing to take us back when we turn away from him too. Just as in our own human relationships, a relationship with God in Christ is a long-term process of understanding. God does not want us to love the idea of him that we have projected from our own feelings, but rather the real God who created the universe and entered into it himself two thousand years ago. The purpose of what might otherwise seem to be theologically tedious documents produced by what some consider senseless (or even sinful) strife, aims to get at just this. Christology matters so that we might be in a right relationship with the God who desires nothing more for us than that we spend the present moment and all future time in his glorious company. And if this isn't a personal relationship, then nothing is.

The fact that God has chosen to relate to us in Jesus has enormous implications for how we live. God is the one who has made the decision, and believing in Jesus is living in the light of this decision on God's part. For this reason, we are sometimes better off translating an important Greek word that St. Paul uses in the Bible (*pistis*) as "faithfulness" rather than "faith" (Galatians 5:22). The latter risks confining our relationship to Jesus to our heads, as if all that matters is what I come to think about him. The former stresses a complete orientation of the self—actions, thoughts, and emotions unified in the desire to emulate and belong to Christ. It may seem a subtle distinction, but it is an important one. It saves me and my feeble brain from having to think or feel rightly all the time. When my head and heart are mixed up, I can still take my body to church, point my eyes toward Holy Scripture, or open my mouth and say a prayer. As my actions remain faithful, I soon discover that my head and heart get back on track as well.

Any married person knows that a successful human relationship must work this way too. I don't always feel "in love," but by fulfilling my various commitments to my wife, my head and heart are filled again with a sense of satisfaction—the knowledge that things are the way they are supposed to be. But the flip side is also true both in everyday human relationships and in my relationship with God in Christ. Sometimes my brain and my feelings are ablaze; but if my actions do not bear witness to my inner state, then what good are they? A man who beats his wife and a woman who cheats on her husband may tell themselves that they love their spouses, but their actions say otherwise. Someone who claims to have a relationship with Jesus but neither worships God nor loves his neighbor cannot be said to have faith (see James 2:14–17).

There's more. The idea of a personal relationship is even richer than a unity of the interior and exterior. As I mentioned, God is the one who initiates the relationship, and in my mind the only way to make sense of how this works is by God's grace, present in the sacraments, in the study of Scripture, and in faithful prayer. After I "received" Jesus as a young child, I wondered for years how it was that I "had" him. Was just thinking fondly about him or piously reminding him of my devotion to him the way that this relationship was meant to unfold until I met him in heaven? This, of course, is a slight parody of my childhood faith; but it reveals a trap into which many have fallen to their peril. In a model like this, it's all about me. And it's *not* about me.

As I began attending the Holy Eucharist, reading the Bible both alone and with others, and learning to pray as Jesus taught his disciples, I discovered union with him that was far more than a feeling. My thoughts and feelings were and are important, but if I wanted to know what a personal relationship with Jesus looked like, I needed to hold him in my hands and take him into my body. I needed to encounter him with my eyes open to the Scriptures and my knees bent in prayer and adoration. As improbable as this seemed to me at first, it became clear to me that the Lord had given me and everyone else the means to "receive" him—once and for all, and on a regular basis. My heart learned to magnify the Lord as Mary's did.

We return to Mary and Pilate. Pilate is stuck in his head, while Mary "treasure[s] all these things in her heart" (Luke 2:51). The Nicene Creed and Chalcedonian Decree are true to Mary in the depths of her being. She gets the "impossible union" through trust and obedience, through fulfilling her appointed obligations unique to all the women who ever lived on earth. She willingly received her Lord for herself and shared him with the world. She had the closest bond with Jesus and shows us how to do the same. Her soul magnified the Lord, while Pilate washed his hands of the whole affair (Matthew 27:24). Right thinking about the union of God and humanity in Jesus ought to place us in the posture of Mary. St. John writes, "Beloved, we are God's children now, and what we will be has not yet appeared; but we know that when he appears we shall be like him, because we shall see him as he is" (1 John 3:2). God's faithfulness to us in Christ makes our spirits rejoice and gives us the deepest assurance that, as St. Athanasius famously said, "God became man so that we might become God."[13] And this profound mystery is the subject of our next chapter.

4

The *Kerygma*

～

"God became man so that we might become God." So says St. Athanasius, one of the great defenders of Christian doctrine in the early Church. When we encounter a statement like this, we realize there remains a lot more to say about Jesus. His identity and work take up more space in both the Apostles' and Nicene Creeds than anything else. And telling his story, more than just pointing out the truth of his two natures, has the power to transform hearts. How does this happen? Because truth matters, we keep exploring.

For many centuries in most parts of the world, the formation of young people primarily meant growing into a cultural and religious identity. It was induction ("leading in") rather than education ("leading out"). To learn anything was to become a more integrated member of society, and thus to

understand oneself. Christians took their cue in this regard
from their spiritual forebears, the Israelites, who were commanded to make the Law of the Lord more than a set of rules.
The Lord, his Law, and the stories of his interaction with his
people were the ground of being. We look once again at the
famous *shema*: *Daily prayer (equivalent to our Father) for Ancient Israelites*

Very influential prayer in Jewish History

Or Listen is translation of Hebrew "Shema"

> "Hear, O Israel: The LORD our God, the LORD is one. You
> shall love the LORD your God with all your heart and
> with all your soul and with all your might. And these
> words that I command you today shall be on your heart.
> You shall teach them diligently to your children, and
> shall talk of them when you sit in your house, and when
> you walk by the way, and when you lie down, and when
> you rise. You shall bind them as a sign on your hand, and
> they shall be as frontlets between your eyes. You shall
> write them on the doorposts of your house and on your
> gates." (Deuteronomy 6:4–9)

Israelites kept their stories fresh in their minds and in their
prayers, notably in the daily recitation of the Psalms. They
even put physical reminders of their faith on their bodies,
homes, and public spaces.

As the Church grew and became "Christendom," the
story of Jesus was meant to work this way in Christian societ-
ies. The twentieth-century German theologian Paul Tillich
states: "One can say that induction was initiation, initiation
into the mystery of human existence."[1] And this mystery
went beyond what ancient Israel knew. It was Israel's story,
combined with its continuation and culmination in the

Messiah. The world has largely forgotten this story. Most of us are shaped by other grand narratives: the various "isms" of political ideology, but also things as mundane as sports and commerce. Fleshing out the story of Jesus, whose identity and work is sketched out in the Apostles' Creed, puts us back on the path to a more satisfying formation. And for most of us, this does mean education—leading out of what ultimately cannot satisfy, and leading into truth, which always does.

But first, death. Jesus "was crucified, died, and was buried," we say in the Apostles' Creed. And he died for something: For you, for me, and for the life of the world. What would you die for? Amid the prosperity of the modern West, it is sometimes hard to imagine dying for anything. Not even military recruiting campaigns emphasize the possibility of death. It is never "Join us and die like those who stormed the beaches of Normandy in 1944," but rather more like "Join us and triumph over the enemies, and then return home to tell us the tale like Grandad did." I have sat with enough dying people to know that most of us are terrified of death to the point of denial. And yet we have a strange longing to give our lives to something worthwhile. Serving in the military wouldn't be such a thrilling prospect if, underneath the positive image of heroism, death weren't a possibility. The problem is, most things aren't worth dying for, but we are dying to live for something that is. And with the failure of every perverted alternative to God's story, a faith worth living and dying for may become ever more attractive in our own age. Paul Tillich describes the terrifying success of Hitler's National Socialism in 1930s Germany in this way:

One could observe how the European youth before the second World War was longing for symbols in which they could see a convincing expression of the meaning of existence. They desired to be initiated into these symbols which demanded unconditional surrender, even if they showed very soon their demonic-destructive character. The young ones wanted something absolutely serious—in contrast to the playing with cultural goods. They wanted something for which they could sacrifice themselves, even if it was a distorted religious-political aim.[2]

The Hitler Youth had an innate longing for the greatest story ever told. In its absence, they were willing to settle for *today?* a nightmare. They were willing to live and die for God, but they lived for and some died for a devil instead.

The story of Jesus does not stop at appreciating the truth of the union of God and man. The earliest Christians did not gather together, worship, and face death simply because they believed in a doctrine of the incarnation of God (true as it is!). In fact, the Christological controversies described in the last chapter make it plain that this was precisely what the earliest Christians needed time to figure out. What they were certain of, however, was what Jesus had done. He was baptized in the Jordan River by his kinsman, John. He resisted Satan's temptations. He walked on water and saved Peter from drowning. He gave sight to the blind, cast out demons, fed thousands of people with a few loaves and fish. He stood in a high place and described what blessedness looked like. He reanimated poor Lazarus. And, as we read in the Bible and affirm in the creeds, he died on a cross and rose again. He appeared in his resurrected body to those who watched him die. Finally, again as we mention explicitly in the creeds, he returned to his heavenly home, where he "is seated at the right hand of the Father." These stories, told by the apostles from the day of Pentecost onward, make up what we call the *kerygma*—the authentic teaching about the good news of God in Jesus. Another word for authentic teaching is "doctrine." The challenge before the apostles was how make this doctrine real to those who weren't there to experience the stories firsthand like they were. Jesus tells Thomas, "Blessed are those who have not seen and yet have believed" (John 20:29). The challenge of understanding and sharing the truth remains just as real for us today.

PETER ON PENTECOST

On the day of Pentecost, when the Holy Spirit was poured out on the disciples, confusion reigned. Not only did people of various ethnicities hear Galileans speaking in their own languages, but it was hard to grasp the significance of the event: "All were amazed and perplexed, saying to one another, 'What does this mean?' But others mocking said, 'They are filled with new wine'" (Acts 2:12–13). The birth of Jesus is the beginning of the story that Peter, speaking in a way not found in the four Gospels, stands up to tell in the second chapter of the book of Acts. The Holy Spirit event is not self-explanatory, and neither is "the Word became flesh" (John 1:14). Countless people beheld Jesus, whom John the Evangelist called glorious, and saw instead an eccentric, a blasphemer, or someone utterly

forgettable. The incarnation of God, therefore, is insufficient by itself to save. God walked the earth, and a lot of people did not care. The Church has taught salvation through faith in Christ for more than two thousand years, and some people simply aren't interested. There must be more. The story must be proclaimed, with no details lacking. The story of Jesus is the story we are called to learn and tell again in our own age.

Peter begins by asserting his sobriety and sanity—not a bad idea for anyone who dares to speak of essential things—and quotes the prophet Joel at length. Peter tells his confused audience the prophecy has been fulfilled. Here's what it's all about:

> "Men of Israel, hear these words: Jesus of Nazareth, a man attested to you by God with mighty works and wonders and signs that God did through him in your midst, as you yourselves know—this Jesus, delivered up according to the definite plan and foreknowledge of God, you crucified and killed by the hands of lawless men. God raised him up, loosing the pangs of death, because it was not possible for him to be held by it." (Acts 2:22–24)

The creedal formula rings through these words. Peter then tells us that Jesus is the heir of King David, who himself acknowledged a greater Lord to come. The end result is that Peter's listeners are "cut to the heart" (Acts 2:36–37) as the Holy Spirit is being poured out on the gathered crowd. They are not told philosophical propositions, but rather their hearts are stirred to receive a story worth living and dying for. They are taught, and they are transformed. They cannot hear

The creeds are the base of knowledge

the *kerygma*—the true story of Jesus—and remain the same. Neither can we. The story that the Apostles' Creed tells us in miniature welcomes us into a much larger program of induction. The outcome is supposed to be that we too are "cut to the heart" by the same gospel that turned a hotheaded Galilean fisherman into a herald of truth.

Peter's listeners inevitably ask what comes next. "Repent and be baptized," Peter tells them (Acts 2:38). In that one day three thousand new members joined what had previously been a tiny inner band of outsiders. A huge crowd suddenly found the most worthy thing of all to live and die for. They knew not only who Jesus was, but what he had done for them and for the whole world. Sadly, we can only imagine how many others heard the *kerygma* that day and chose against it.

BLESSED ARE . . .

Those who choose in favor of the authentic preaching and teaching of Jesus may not always do so consciously. In fact, the deeper it soaks into a person, the less it belongs to the realm of the intellect. God wants all of you and asks you to surrender your whole self to him, so that he may make you new. This surrender certainly includes your conscious mind; but this part of a person can easily become a stumbling block to true understanding. Some of us overthink.

When Jesus offers his own authentic teaching, he is normally more interested in being *descriptive* than *prescriptive*. He wants to tell us what those who belong to him and his kingdom are like. The best distillation of this teaching is in what is known in Matthew's Gospel as the Sermon on the Mount (Matthew 5–7), and in Luke's Gospel as the Sermon on the Plain (Luke 6:17–49). Both Gospels contain his blessings, the famous Beatitudes, albeit in slightly different versions; but Matthew's account contains much more besides. An important part of the authentic teaching of Jesus that must be mentioned, however, is how we arrive at his great kerygmatic moment that contains the Beatitudes. Here we remember the last chapter's insistence upon the true incarnation of God—the beginning of the saving work of Christ, that includes the teachings that he will offer with unique authority as the God-man.

When Jesus sits in the midst of his disciples on top of the mountain, he does so in two special capacities. On the one hand, he is the new Moses, as foretold by the old Moses (Deuteronomy 18:17–18)—a portrait that Matthew is careful to paint for us from the very beginning of his Gospel. To escape Herod's murderous designs on the male children of Bethlehem, Jesus's family flees to Egypt, creating a thematic and geographic link with Moses, who also survived infanticide. Jesus, like Moses, experiences exile in the wilderness in response to an undeniable call (Moses at the burning bush, Jesus at his baptism). Finally, Moses ascended Mount Sinai to receive the Law of God—the Torah—and returned to give it to the people. Jesus's Sermon on the Mount is his description of what a fulfilled Law of Moses looks like, intensifying the commands of the Lord given through Moses: "You have heard that it was said . . . but I say. . . ."

"I say." Moses taught only what was from God, and Jesus does too. But Jesus is no mere messenger. He is not just a prophet. He is the incarnate God who gave Moses the Law in the first place. When Jesus teaches, he teaches as God. And what does he teach? He describes those who have ingested the *kerygma*, the truth: the poor in spirit, those who mourn, the meek, those who are hungry and thirsty for righteousness, those who are merciful, those who are pure in heart, peacemakers, the persecuted, and those who are reviled and falsely accused on account of him (Matthew 5:3–11). Only these people, who have pinned their hopes to God's reality and therefore find nothing else satisfying, have cause to rejoice (5:12).

What Jesus teaches us has nothing to do with our working harder to achieve some holy end, as if the Beatitudes were a spurring-on to be more merciful, pure in heart, and so on. Again, Jesus is describing, not prescribing. Hence the Law intensifies, not lessens. It is not enough to follow a rule that says not to kill. What matters is that your heart would find taking someone's life simply impossible. It is not enough to follow a rule that says not to cheat on your wife. Again, would your heart even entertain such a thing? This may sound like absurd perfectionism (Matthew 5:48), but it is really just trusting in a perfect God. Only God is perfect, but certain markers of our character bear witness to the fact that our faith is real. When we look out at the world and both weep for its brokenness and shout for joy at its potential for glorification, the kingdom of heaven has come near indeed. The *kerygma* is living and true. We prove that we have been taught the truth.

The Beatitudes, not to mention the parables of Jesus, remind us once again that we are characters in God's story, not the other way around. In Christ, we are not simply inspired to do good things, or get refreshment for our self-esteem. Christian doctrine gives no license for us to think of God as a combination superhero and therapist in the sky, swooping down as a last resort to fix our problems. Nor is God simply trying to force us into an arbitrary way of living. He is offering us adoption, and this is what his story is about at every turn of the page. Wrapping up the Sermon on the Mount, Jesus says of our final judgment, when he will offer himself to us once and for all as Lord:

> "On that day many will say to me, 'Lord, Lord, did we not prophesy in your name, and cast out demons in your name, and do many mighty works in your name?' And then I will declare to them, 'I never knew you; depart from me, you workers of lawlessness.'" (Matthew 7:21–23)

Lawlessness. Imagine that. Trying to do what God wants may, in the end, have the opposite of its intended effect. The expanded doctrine of the Nicene Creed hammers this home all the time: God made me through his Word, his Word became flesh, suffered, died to take away the sins of the world, rose again to defeat death forever, and returned to heaven. All that remains for me is to be transformed by the reality that the authentic story of God in Jesus Christ conveys. My task, like those on the day of Pentecost in ancient Jerusalem is to be "cut to the heart," repent and believe, over and over again (Acts 2:37).[3]

NICODEMUS

In the European Enlightenment of the eighteenth century, belief was frowned upon by the elite. The *kerygma* became an unlikely if not silly story, and doctrine seemed dry and dead. Happily, we seem to be in an age now that has moved beyond the idolatry of rationalism. The "new atheism" that dominated best-seller lists in the early years of the present century has quietly fizzled out; but we are no nearer to mainstream orthodoxy than we were one hundred (or five hundred!) years ago. In fact, while outright atheism may not be as prevalent in the United States as it is elsewhere, "no religion" or hybrid spiritualities proliferate widely. Complete indifference to faith may be the greatest problem of all. But there is every reason to believe that with zealous preaching and teaching like that of Peter, John Chrysostom, St. Dominic, and John Wesley, the *kerygma* is as likely to succeed in our own day just as it did with superabundance on Pentecost. It may succeed more subtly and gradually as well. The New Testament provides examples of this kind of discovery of truth.

A number of Jesus's conversations in the Gospels give profound insight into how to tell his story. In fact, they are more than conversations. They are moments of true relationship, touchstones of truth rising out of both wisdom and compassion. Nicodemus, who first appears in chapter 3 of John's Gospel, may be the premier example. First, we learn that Nicodemus "came to Jesus by night" (John 3:2). He represents so many truth-seekers in our own day, ashamed or worried for various reasons that their hunger for the living God will be found out. They know that the values the world has imposed upon them are bankrupt, but they are not sure where else to turn. As a forerunner of today's seekers, Nicodemus is curiously abashed to regard as inadequate the answers he has grown accustomed to believing. He treads carefully down the path to truth and transformation. He is "a man of the Pharisees . . . a ruler of the Jews" (John 3:1), and he tells Jesus respectable things for someone of his station. Nicodemus can concede without controversy that Jesus is a rabbi, a teacher who has come from God, and a man who works wonders (John 3:2). How many in our own day are more than happy to assent to such a description of Jesus, but nothing more?

Jesus, however, is not interested in being thought of as a godly exemplar. He pushes Nicodemus to go deeper, and not by talking at him. Jesus reaches his heart. Nicodemus must be born again of water and the Spirit, and this is the difficult part for the mind to grasp. The old Nicodemus must die with the Messiah—the end result of believing the unseen truth of God's saving plan. The rational mind of our own day, as in Nicodemus's, balks at such a challenge. Be born again? But the challenge of the *kerygma*, the truth of Jesus's life and work, is that it compromises even the "truth" of things we have come to see and know by experience. Jesus reminds Nicodemus that it is no more mysterious a thing to be born a second time spiritually than it was for him to be born a first time physically. The essential story of Jesus's incarnation, life, death, resurrection, and ascension may seem like easy prey for rationalist predators, but it is no more extraordinary a story than the ones our world claims to know all about. Why Jesus rose from the dead and promises us the same is no easier to comprehend than why life exists in the world at all. Why is it so scandalous that we could live forever, and yet perfectly "natural" that we live for eighty or ninety years?

Jesus's encounter with Nicodemus reminds us that there is nothing irrational about faith. God's truth has seemingly extraordinary elements, but when we think hard about what we consider "ordinary," we find there really is no such thing. The world that has made perfect sense to Nicodemus eventually makes no sense without Jesus. At some undetermined point, his earnest seeking has become ardent belief. He literally finds his part to play in the authentic teaching of Jesus, no longer coming to Jesus "by night" (John 19:39) but assisting openly with the pious preparation of Jesus's body for burial. We hear of no fireworks or fanfare as he comes around to the truth. In fact, we remain in the dark about his faith journey until encountering him again in John's Gospel (sixteen chapters later) as a committed disciple. He comes to belong to God's story, and he shows us a way of embracing Jesus and his message as well.

DOUBT

Coming to faith in Jesus is almost never a simple assent to the facts of a story, however likely. On the one hand, many of us find the witness of the apostles overwhelmingly convincing. They had the authority to share the *kerygma* and pass it down for us to do the same because they were there when it happened. The culmination of Peter's kerygmatic speech on

Pentecost leaves a deep impression: "This Jesus God raised up, and of that we all are witnesses" (Acts 2:32). Peter insists on this point again in another inspired moment (the crucial scene when the earliest Church understands how to include non-Jews within the fellowship):

> And we are witnesses of all that he did both in the country of the Jews and in Jerusalem. They put him to death by hanging him on a tree, but God raised him on the third day and made him to appear, not to all the people but to us who had been chosen by God as witnesses, who ate and drank with him after he rose from the dead. And he commanded us to preach to the people and to testify that he is the one appointed by God to be judge of the living and the dead. (Acts 10:39–42)

There are a chosen few who see, but most do not. And we all know that eyewitness accounts differ. A crowd of people who behold the same spectacle will invariably tell the same story in many different ways. And we have all had the sense, even when being a firsthand witness to something, that our eyes may deceive us. Many people have experienced miracles and walked away from them in disbelief. Many more have heard someone else's description of something extraordinary and dismissed it as a misunderstanding, a joke, a raving, or at best a deeply personal "truth" that need not or should not infect anyone else.

The end of Matthew's Gospel, without critique or commentary, reminds us that even those who stood alongside the risen Jesus were uncertain:

Now the eleven disciples went to Galilee, to the mountain to which Jesus had directed them. And when they saw him they worshiped him, but some doubted. (Matthew 28:16–17)

The resurrection account in Luke's Gospel reflects the same uncertainty: Mary Magdalene, Joanna, and Mary (the mother of James) find the tomb empty and report back to the other disciples, "but these words seemed to them an idle tale, and they did not believe them" (Luke 24:11). When it comes to faith, hearing is not always believing—and neither is seeing. Mary Magdalene sees the risen Christ in John 20 and mistakes him at first for a gardener. Her heart is opened to receive the risen Christ when he speaks her name, proving that God always makes the first move. Luke's story of the road to Emmaus makes a similar point with even more mysterious drama (Luke 24:13–35). Once again, we learn that faith does not begin with us, but with God. Once again, we are slapped in the face with the reality of God's story refashioning our own. Once again, we stand helpless trying to make any progress in the narrative without God's authorial control.

The story of the disciples on the road to Emmaus speaks powerfully to how one receives the authentic teachings about who Jesus is and what he did. They are terribly confused, but at least they are on the right road. These two know a lot of the story, because they've just lived through it. Their minds are flooded with details but they cannot discern the truth standing in front of them. In fact, they begin unwittingly to tell Jesus his own story. They are grasping in the darkness of ignorance in the presence of light. It turns out to be exactly the right thing to do. Jesus takes over:

> "O foolish ones, and slow of heart to believe all that the prophets have spoken! Was it not necessary that the Christ should suffer these things and enter into his glory?" And beginning with Moses and all the Prophets, he interpreted to them in all the Scriptures the things concerning himself. (Luke 24:25–27)

Jesus speeds up their slow hearts and quickens their dull minds; but still something is missing. So they don't let Jesus go. They invite him to supper, and he celebrates Holy Communion with them:

> When he was at table with them, he took the bread and blessed and broke it and gave it to them. And their eyes were opened, and they recognized him. (Luke 24:30–31)

The heart of faith sees only what has been revealed, and the disciples recognize the risen Jesus in this instance only in the form of a sacrament. It is no one-off miracle, but a template for faith formation down through the centuries. Conversion is not taking a salvation pill, but beginning a lifelong treatment program. The disciples' earnest seeking pays big rewards from the storehouse of God's revealing grace.

In St. Paul's words:

> having the eyes of your hearts enlightened . . . you may know what is the hope to which he has called you, what

are the riches of his glorious inheritance in the saints, and what is the immeasurable greatness of his power toward us who believe, according to the working of his great might that he worked in Christ when he raised him from the dead and seated him at his right hand in the heavenly places. (Ephesians 1:18–20)

"The eyes of your hearts": This is where the truth comes home to us, and it brings us back to the notion of education out of old ways and induction into God's ways. God's grace makes his story true over time in the depth of our being, and we see our present and future role within it. Only then does a likely story become the story worth dying for.

One further biblical example of conversion reinforces our point. The end of John's Gospel makes it clear that Thomas was chief among these doubters who came to hear the Great Commission (Matthew 28:16–20). Peter and John have amazingly come to believe by seeing the empty tomb. Mary Magdalene, as we mentioned, does not recognize Jesus at first, but quickly becomes the first eyewitness to the resurrection. Thomas will not believe without seeing; nor will he believe only by seeing. Unlike Mary Magdalene, he does not mistake what his eyes see for someone or something else. But for all he knows, there is another explanation: a ghost? He declares:

"Unless I see in his hands the mark of the nails, and place my finger into the mark of the nails, and place my hand into his side, I will never believe." (John 20:25)

Thomas lives for eight days in this skeptical state. Jesus finally appears again to his disciples, and (somewhat surprisingly) he allows Thomas to dispel his doubt on his own terms: "Put your finger here" (John 20:27). The result is the highest praise of Jesus to be found anywhere in the four Gospel accounts: "My Lord, and my God!" (John 20:28).

Occasionally God not only quickens slow hearts but revives dead ones. God not only engages with our skepticism (as in Jesus's encounter with Nicodemus) but indulges it for the sake of an even more profound transformation. In a sense, some get to see and believe (and even touch) so that the rest of us may believe without seeing.

THE MAIN CHARACTER EMERGES

So far we have kept in the background what must now come to the fore: the Holy Spirit. The delivery and reception of the *kerygma* is, after all, invariably the Holy Spirit's work. "And we are witnesses to these things," St. Peter says yet again in the Acts of the Apostles, but "so is the Holy Spirit, whom God has given to those who obey him" (5:32). It is the Holy Spirit who descends upon Peter and the other disciples on Pentecost, and the Holy Spirit who transforms Peter into the man who can stand up and preach the gospel. In Acts 2, those who hear and believe Peter receive the same Holy Spirit that has moved him to speak. This pattern repeats again and again, as we see in Acts 10, when the inspired apostle shares the *kerygma* with Gentiles in the home of Cornelius and the

Holy Spirit descends on the crowd while Peter is still talking (10:44).

It is the Holy Spirit who moved over the waters in creation and sustains all life now. It is the Holy Spirit whom a Christian receives in baptism (1 Corinthians 12:13) when he is buried with Christ in his death and raised with Christ in his glory (Romans 6:3–5). It is the Holy Spirit who educates and inducts; and it is the Holy Spirit whose story we must now explore more fully.

Should people recieve the fullness of the Holy Spirit prior to any catechesis?.

5

The Fire Within

An old minister in my community told me a story about the greatest sermon he had ever preached. It was Easter Sunday morning, and the moment had come for him to ascend the pulpit. In the two steps between his seat and the pulpit, he believed he heard a voice telling him, "Not that one." He abandoned his manuscript and decided to wing it. His words were spontaneous, but not one of them was out of place.

In an instant, nothing seemed right about the careful crafting he had done to prepare for the biggest day in the church's year. All he could hear was, "Not that one." What my minister friend was responding to was that feeling we get in our gut—one that we too often ignore but know we shouldn't. It isn't so much a sense of right and wrong as a desire within us to offer something real. What this old preacher experienced was the Holy Spirit. And this man believes in the Holy Spirit.

But what happened? Was he zapped from out of nowhere? Not at all. In fact, he responded to what had long been within him and around him. He was guided, gifted, and comforted by an active God who is not content to be relegated to "up there." In fact, the God whose story we have explored so far is the God within the heart (or gut)[1] of everyone he has claimed to be a part of his kingdom. And the key concept to keep straight right from the start as we think about the Holy Spirit is precisely that the Holy Spirit is God. He is a person of the Holy Trinity: the Holy Spirit is not just a feeling or an energy that we can somehow channel, but the constant companion within us and all around us who is waiting at every moment for us to respond to his call. My minister friend acknowledged God, and his story took a wonderfully unexpected turn into God's story.

ASK THE GOD-MAN

Jesus is Emmanuel, "God with us," and he is indeed with us. He reigns over us in his resurrected body in heaven and he has left us as his Body, the Church, in which he continues to give himself for the life of the world (John 6:33). But before his ascension into heaven, he promised his disciples that he would not leave them alone, that another advocate or comforter would come to be with them until the end of the age. Jesus tells us, "the Helper, the Holy Spirit, whom the father will send in my name, he will teach you all things and bring to your remembrance all that I have said to you" (John 14:26; cf. 15:26). In other words, the way in which Jesus, who always shows us the Father, is still present in the world is through the Holy Spirit. Once again, the three-personed God is always at work, united in essence and operation. What Jesus left his followers is nothing less than the very love that flows from before the beginning of time between the Father and the Son, the love which, as we read in the book of Colossians, "binds everything together in perfect harmony" (3:14). The Holy Spirit, then, is God actively bringing together and binding what is his. The Holy Spirit is how God's story is my story, and how my story is part of the story of the people of God.

Although the Holy Spirit was given to the Church to be fundamentally uniting, we have frequently proven to be confused in our understanding of this divine gift. Many of the Church's attempts to develop a doctrine of the Holy Spirit have been controversial. The Spirit has his own biblical history and theological legacy. We can see the Christian community at Corinth seeking to figure out the truth in the pages of the New Testament. They seem to be missing the point of God's presence among them by arguing over who is authentically Spirit-filled. "No one can say 'Jesus is Lord,'" Paul says, "except in the Holy Spirit" (1 Corinthians 12:3). There are no super-Christians. No follower of Jesus has a larger share of the Holy Spirit than anyone else. We shall return to this concern as we address some practical contemporary matters at the end of this chapter.

The Bible says a lot of things about the Holy Spirit; but the vast content can be boiled down to the three times the

Holy Spirit comes up in the Gospel according to Mark. A slippery surface requires some traction, and the shortest, most straightforward of the four Gospel books may provide it here. First, John the Baptist contrasts his ministry to Jesus's with specific reference to the Holy Spirit: "I have baptized you with water, but he will baptize you with the Holy Spirit" (Mark 1:8). Matthew and Luke put the same words on John's lips with one addition: "and fire" (Matthew 3:11; Luke 3:16). St. Jerome (ca. 345–ca. 419), who translated the Scriptures into Latin, describes the difference between a baptism of mere water and one of the Holy Spirit in this way:

> No baptism can be called perfect except that which depends on the cross and resurrection of Christ.[2]

St. Paul says it like this:

> Do you not know that all of us who have been baptized into Christ Jesus were baptized into his death? We were buried therefore with him by baptism into death, in order that, just as Christ was raised from the dead by the glory of the Father, we too might walk in newness of life.
>
> For if we have been united with him in a death like his, we shall certainly be united with him in a resurrection like his. (Romans 6:3–5)

We cannot talk about the Holy Spirit without circling back to talk about the cross and the empty tomb. Here the "fire" of Matthew and Luke amplifies what Mark has said more simply. Because of the saving work of Jesus, God continues to operate throughout his creation until the final consummation of his work of new creation (see chapter 8). When we are baptized we don't just wash off sins, but by the power of the Holy Spirit we put on the divine nature of the Holy Trinity. This, then, is what the Holy Spirit is. He is not a thing. He is not really something I acquire. He is a person—the special means of my participation in God's love for me and for the world. And this participation should be a raging fire if there ever was one.[3]

And so we come upon Jesus's second word about the Holy Spirit in Mark's Gospel: "Whoever blasphemes against the Holy Spirit never has forgiveness, but is guilty of an eternal sin" (3:29). A literary illustration may help us here. In C. S. Lewis's Chronicles of Narnia, the four Pevensie children (Peter, Susan, Edmund, and Lucy) enter a new world through the wardrobe of an old house in the English countryside. There they meet talking animals, and most prominent among them is Aslan who, like Jesus, "isn't safe. But he's good. He's the king."[4] The four children eventually reign as kings and queens in Aslan's stead for many years, until by chance they rediscover the old wardrobe and find themselves once again children in England. They return to the very moment when they left. They have experienced many years in one dimension and no time at all in another. Afterward, the children return to Narnia on a number of occasions; but eventually one of the four, Susan, loses interest. When the final battle for Narnia comes, Susan is not there. The reality that she inhabited for a lifetime is no longer the reality she desires. She has immatured, and there is a tragedy about her choice. She is left out of Aslan's country, presumably forever.

As Rowan Williams writes, "The price of encountering reality, we might say, is precisely the recognition that there isn't any alternative to it."[5] Once I am a participant in the life of God, there is no turning back. Once I have the fire, it is absurd to imagine I could put it out.

Now, on the one hand, the question of who is saved is always a mystery, and we shall explore the doctrines surrounding this mystery in the next chapter. On the other hand, the Bible makes it clear that there is such a thing as an ultimate decision in favor of or against the God of grace and truth. Sinning against the Holy Spirit is rejecting my part in the story of God. It is denying the new nature that has replaced the one that was leading me nowhere. It is declaring myself God. It is to say that the whole dynamic of repentance and forgiveness is nonsense, that I do not need saving, and I am just fine the way I am. All who have received the Holy Spirit run the risk of betrayal; but an occasional "Not that one" has a way of setting our hearts straight. Imagine yourself standing before the Lord and being told "Not that one" about all kinds of things you may have done, said, or thought. If just reading that last sentence creates a desire in you to be rid of whatever separates you from God, then you have every reason to believe you are not and will not be a blasphemer against the Holy Spirit. You desire to live in Narnia in the way that Susan Pevensie does not.

In our third instance from Mark's Gospel, we find Jesus describing the Holy Spirit's effect in our daily lives:

> "And when they bring you to trial and deliver you over,
> do not be anxious beforehand what you are to say, but say

whatever is given you in that hour, for it is not you who speak, but the Holy Spirit." (Mark 13:11)

If there was ever a story of someone living for a moment as if Jesus's promise were true, it is my old minister friend. "Not that one." Jesus is talking more immediately about the persecution that his followers will face; but like all of his words, they resonate more deeply through the centuries, and we apply them to countless circumstances. If it's all up to me to think of and try to articulate the truth, what good am I to anybody? But if it is God inspiring me and speaking through me, then the world is on notice. God does not just sit inside me forbidding me to betray him. He is at work. And the work of God within me is always and only happening in the present moment, not the past or the future. We rely again on C. S. Lewis, who puts it this way in another book:

In a word, the Future is, of all things, the thing least like eternity. It is the most completely temporal part of time—for the Past is frozen and no longer flows, and the Present is all lit up with eternal rays.[6]

The Holy Spirit is not interested in imaginary conversations in which I construct what I would have said to that jerk who wouldn't give me a chance to speak. The Holy Spirit is not an antiquarian, carrying me back in my mind to an imagined glory day. The Holy Spirit is not about "What if?" The Holy Spirit is with us now. Right now!

THE FIRE

There is much more to say about how the Holy Spirit works among us. Let us see now how the Holy Spirit functions in a human life—how the third person of the Holy Trinity, the very presence of God that we find in the very first story of the Bible— governs us from the inside out. The seventeenth-century Anglican bishop Jeremy Taylor (d. 1667) describes it beautifully:

> God is especially present in the hearts of His people, by His Holy Spirit: and indeed the hearts of holy men are temples in the truth of things, and in type and shadow they are heaven itself.[7]

"Temples in the truth of things." Taylor gives clarity to one of the things we say about the Holy Spirit in the Nicene Creed—namely, that the Spirit "has spoken through the Prophets." First of all we recognize the truth spoken and captured in the pages of Scripture by the recognized prophets of Israel (Isaiah, Jeremiah, Ezekiel, Amos, Hosea, et al.). But second, and most important for our daily lives, we recognize that the truth—God's Word written on our hearts—is within us, and that the Holy Spirit is bringing it out. In this way, the apostle Paul was much more interested in the quality of the Corinthians' prophesying (a synonym in Paul's mind for saying true things) than he was with their speaking in tongues. He argues:

> For one who speaks in a tongue speaks not to men but to God; for no one understands him, but he utters mysteries

in the Spirit. On the other hand, the one who prophesies speaks to people for their upbuilding and encouragement and consolation. (1 Corinthians 14:2–3)

Prophesying was and is truth telling, not gazing into a crystal ball. It is sharing insight that only God the Holy Spirit can elicit from our hearts and minds.

My old preacher friend believed that God's truth flowed out of him. It is not unreasonable to assume he was right. As we saw in the last chapter, that very thing happened to St. Peter in Acts 2. Peter was as close to Jesus as anyone, and yet denied him three times (John 18:15–27). Peter was later redeemed when he told Jesus he loved him three times; but the Gospels show us a man who was both deeply faithful and deeply conflicted. Right up to the end, he was confused about who Jesus was. We can only imagine how he must have felt after Jesus disappeared again into heaven. And then it was Pentecost—and with the coming of the Holy Spirit, Peter suddenly stood up with full spiritual stature and opened full blast with the words of the Lord himself, laying out the *kerygma* (discussed in the last chapter). Peter's words brought three thousand people into the fold. Did he expect that? Whatever was on his mind, whatever he would usually say, whatever he was able to do on his own simply disappeared: "Not that one," my preacher friend would say. With the Holy Spirit within us, we are capable of the same extraordinary acts, despite our many flaws.

So how do we get the Holy Spirit? How does an ordinary Christian wind up in the same place as Peter? How does the Holy Spirit make us a new person, and "not that one"?

Christians have believed for many long centuries that the gateway that leads to our receiving the Holy Spirit is the sacrament of baptism. Baptism and the faith to which baptism points is the starting point for the New Testament's discussion of the Holy Spirit, and it is our starting point too. Again, let's recall Acts 2 and Pentecost: It is primarily a sound event. It is a call. We think often about the wind and the fire in the story of Pentecost, the coming of the Holy Spirit. But what does the Bible actually say?

> And suddenly there came from heaven *a sound like a mighty rushing wind*, and it filled the entire house where they were sitting. And divided tongues as of fire appeared to them and rested on each one of them. (Acts 2:2–3, emphasis added)

There is memorable visual imagery, but what comes first is the sound, the call. This call is violent, and it shakes everything up, "like a mighty rushing wind" (Acts 2:2). We may not even be able to comprehend it, but that is what happens to each of us as we are sprinkled or dunked with water, and the Trinitarian formula is pronounced over us (Matthew 28:19). We are called and shaken violently to new life. And then the process begins as we make our way through the rest of our natural lives to hear that call again, and again, and again. This call came to Noah, whom God asked to build a boat in the face of people who thought he was crazy. This call came to Abram and Sarai who became parents in their old age and served as the foundation of God's chosen people. This call came to Moses who encountered God in fire on Mount

Sinai and descended again with the Law by which God would have his people live. This call came to Jesus himself, who at his baptism was claimed by the Father as the beloved one in whom he is well pleased (Matthew 3:17; Mark 1:11; Luke 3:22; cf. 2 Peter 1:17). In our baptism we are adopted as sons and daughters too. In the Holy Spirit, our new nature is that of being beloved in the sight of God. We are called into a life of well-pleasing listening to the continual call to abandon all that conflicts with God's will for our lives and the life of the world. "Not that one."

And more follows. Those of us who have received the Holy Spirit in baptism—who have been shaken by that initial call—may hear dramatic, ecstatic, exuberant calling again in our lives. But we also know life isn't usually like that. We who experience dramatic events also experience a lot of quietness and silence. God is always there, but are we still listening even when the violent, rushing wind has died down and the tongues of flame have faded away? A good example here is the story of the prophet Elijah. God is not present to Elijah in the earthquake. God is not present to Elijah in the wind, nor in the fire. There is no drama. There is no excitement. For Elijah and for us, God is found in the "sound of sheer silence" (1 Kings 19:12 NRSV), or as the King James Bible puts it, "in the still small voice" of God.

All of us who have the Holy Spirit and who have moments of ecstasy in our relationship with God also have lots of quiet time, lots of silence. Do we waste it? Do we just imagine that those are everyday times? Or do we treat those like Pentecost moments too? For those who have never been Christians and have felt their whole lives to be evidence of God's silence, perhaps it has been instead an invitation. In either case, all moments are God moments. There is no person whom he is not calling, and there is no moment when the call isn't coming. If the experience of God was only about rushing winds and tongues of flame, we would be akin to spiritual drug addicts—languishing in painfully ordinary times until the next Holy Spirit fix. But Christians believe in the Holy Spirit—God—who is always active now, not just in some exciting moment to come.

"NOT THAT ONE" REDUX

This is a book about why truth matters, and we have so far sketched a doctrine of the Holy Spirit that the Church has long held to be true: the Holy Spirit is God. And indeed, this simple statement is about all that the earliest Christians could say. In the Apostles' Creed, the Holy Spirit is mentioned in just two ways:

1. "He was conceived by the power of the Holy Spirit."[8]
2. "I believe in the Holy Spirit."

That's it.

By the time of the Council of Constantinople of 381, which was a sort of the second part of the Council of Nicaea (see chapter 2), it was necessary to say more. There is just too much about the Holy Spirit in the Bible to fit into these two doctrinal places. At the Council of Constantinople, almost sixty years after the Council of Nicaea, the doctrine of the Holy Spirit was expanded. This formula (with one controversial addition coming later) is what most Christians profess down to the present day:

> We believe in the Holy Spirit, the Lord, the giver of life, who proceeds from the Father *[and the Son]*. With the Father and the Son he is worshiped and glorified. He has spoken through the prophets.

I say most Christians because of what you see in brackets. That's the controversial addition. It is a long and complicated story that need not be told in full here; but eventually Christians in Western Europe began adding the words *and the Son* to the Creed where it had not originally been. To this day, Eastern Orthodox Christians reject this change.

"And the Son" made its way into the Nicene-Constantinopolitan Creed as a way to reteach the Christian faith to groups that had been evangelized by Arians, particularly in German-speaking lands. (The persistence of the Arians, by the way, is a stark reminder that heresies do not simply go away!) In any case, orthodox Christians were looking for a way to strengthen the idea of the divinity of Jesus ("through whom all things were made") among those who had a long tradition of regarding Jesus as a creature (see chapter 2). But orthodox believers remembered a key passage of Scripture, when Jesus appears to the disciples in his resurrected body. He twice pronounces his peace and declares, "As the Father has sent me, even so I am sending you" (John 20:21). Then we read

And when he had said this, he breathed on them and said
to them, "Receive the Holy Spirit. If you forgive the sins
of any, they are forgiven them; if you withhold forgiveness from any, it is withheld." (John 20:22–23)

Of course, as we have already noted, the Holy Spirit has
everything to do with Jesus; but what did it mean to say that
the Holy Spirit proceeded not only from the Father (as in the
original creed) but also "and the Son" (Latin, *filioque*)? There
is a centuries-long story about the back-and-forth between
East and West over defining these terms.[9] There were strong
theological arguments mounted both in favor of and against
adding filioque to the Creed. In the East, it sounded better
to say that the Spirit proceeded through the Son (if it was
necessary to say anything at all), in the same way that the
Father created everything through the Word. "From the Son"
sounded a bit too much like in the beginning there were two
(Father and Son) who made a third (the Spirit). In the end,
however, the issue that seemed most troubling in the East was
that there would be any tampering with the Creed at all. The
Council of Nicaea (amplified by the Council of Constantinople) had decided, and no regional church could just change
something that the whole body of the faithful had agreed
upon. The result was the tragic separation of the Eastern
churches from the Western churches around the middle of
the eleventh century.

MODALISM

The dispute over whether the Holy Spirit proceeds just from the Father or from both the Father and the Son continues among people who, for the most part, recognize each other as genuine brothers and sisters in Christ. Depending on whom you ask, disagreement about this question may not even fall under the category of "heresy" (again, depending on whom you ask!). But there is an older and more pressing heresy related to the Holy Spirit that we must sketch out briefly, and it brings us back to my old minister friend. This heresy is called modalism, with a particularly popular flavor of it called Sabellianism (after Sabellius, ca. 225). It is an easy trap to fall into.

As we have explored already, heresies are usually easier than the truth, but they are less satisfying in the end. If the earliest Christians had been modalists instead of trinitarians, they would have had a lot more to say about the Holy Spirit right from the start. According to this view, Father, Son, and Holy Spirit are different ways in which God reveals himself. These are simply different guises or ways of being—different forms or modes, almost akin to states of matter. It is a popular default position even among Christian preachers and teachers who do not think they are championing anything wrong. But they are, and it matters. A modalist, for example, would view my preacher friend's experience of "Not that one" in a completely different way than we have described. God would simply be zapping him with an experience, not eliciting truth out of the depth of his heart. To a modalist, the Holy Spirit mostly comes and goes, unbound by a substantial identity (or divine eternal personality) as the true and living God. To a modalist, the Holy Spirit can be used as a prop to describe how God is doing new things, even where the new things contradict the old things. If the Holy Spirit is just an energetic guise of God, then anything I experience could be (or not!) the work of the Holy Spirit. To an orthodox trinitarian, however, the Holy Spirit is doing in me and my community only what is true, revealed for all time to God's people throughout time and space. That is why the Nicene-Constantinopolitan Creed carefully chose to say of the Holy Spirit: "giver of life . . . proceeds . . . worshiped and glorified . . . spoken through the Prophets." Theologian Justin Holcomb describes the choice of orthodox doctrine of the Holy Spirit over modalism:

> Trinitarian theology is much more than a merely human philosophy. It takes seriously the idea that God has revealed himself in Scripture and wants to be known, and that he has revealed himself in a certain way.[10]

Christian doctrine dismisses modalism, because modalism creates the need for a true God behind the three masks. How does this God work? Is there another God behind this one? Where does the regression end? Modalism flies in the face of the revealed record of God and his people that we are insisting is the grand narrative into which Christians are initiated. The One to whom Jesus cries out on the cross is the very One who, through the Word, spoke everything that is into existence. Doctrine that moves beyond the simple "I believe in the Holy Spirit" shows how this is so, and as long as we operate with a working theology of the Holy Spirit as something akin to a magic force that comes and goes, we may actually find ourselves sinning against him. Put another way, if the doctrinal structure of the Holy Spirit is faulty, everything else comes crashing down around it. Truth matters.

PENTECOSTALISM

I mentioned earlier that if we proceed in our faith with a false understanding of the Holy Spirit as God, we may end up something like spiritual junkies. Modalism lends itself to this life. If the Holy Spirit is more like an unpredictable zap of God's power than an intractable presence of God around and within me from the moment of my baptism, then faith is necessarily a wearisome scheme of highs and lows. In some respects, this is the reality captured by Pentecostalism, a twentieth-century religious movement that has won enormous numbers of converts worldwide. Many Christian groups are explicitly Pentecostal, but many more have incorporated elements of Pentecostalism that remain part of the fabric of different Christian traditions. To say that those with Pentecostal credentials care about the Holy Spirit would be an understatement.

Something like Pentecostalism was bound to happen, and it is not entirely at odds with received Christian doctrine. In Acts 19, St. Paul comes to Ephesus and finds some disciples. He asks, "Did you receive the Holy Spirit when you believed?" They reply, "No, we have not even heard that there is a Holy Spirit" (v. 2). Closer to our own day, as the world became industrialized, rationalistic, and sure of its own progress,

fewer people imagined a God who creates and sustains everything that happens on earth. Much of the religion that survived the Enlightenment and made its way into the modern
age was, like the age itself, devoid of deep mystery. Some
Christians began to wonder, like Paul, if their nominal brethren had ever heard of the Holy Spirit at all. But Paul's problem
is that the Ephesians he encounters had not been baptized
correctly. Apollos, who had baptized these Ephesians, only
seems to have known about the preparatory baptism of John
the Baptist, Jesus's forerunner (Acts 18:24–19:7; cf. Matthew
3:1–12). Apollos's followers may have not fully understood
the implications of Jesus's resurrection, and therefore had not
received once and for all the gift that would animate their
lives and govern all that they do for Christ and for his kingdom. It isn't just that they weren't excited enough about God
or reporting enough electrifying activity in their worship
meetings.

Contemporary Pentecostals take St. Paul's concern much
further, falling at times into modalist spiritual sickness. For
them, the initiation of Christian life by trinitarian baptism
and faith in the good news of Christ is not enough. There is a
completely separate practice in which a person asks for—and
so it is believed—receives the "baptism of the Holy Spirit" (a
spiritual benefit not associated with baptism or conversion).
Within this tradition, this "second work of grace" is very
commonly accompanied by the gift of speaking in tongues.
It is not unusual within some Pentecostal churches for those
who cannot exhibit this gift to be treated like second-class
Christians. There is here a substantial failure to grasp and to
practice the teaching of the apostle in 1 Corinthians 12–14.

Some of the same errors which Paul sought to correct in first-century Corinth are reasserted in present-day churches. Speaking in tongues is not a requirement for being a Christian, and has proved an exceedingly rare (but real) spiritual gift. Thankfully Paul's teaching on the Holy Spirit and spiritual gifts insists that all Christians in one Spirit have been "baptized into the body of Christ—Jews or Greeks, slaves or free—and all made to drink of one Spirit," whether they spoke in tongues or not (1 Corinthians 12:12–13, 27–31). And while speaking in tongues is clearly a biblical gift, feeling spiritual ecstasy, falling down, and having out-of-body sensations are presupposed nowhere in Scripture and are never advocated by the fathers of the Church.

But even if we reject the excesses of Pentecostalism, too many Christians do minimize the Holy Spirit, thereby ignoring the hope of glory inherent in Christ's work within us. In this way, we are once again living in a state of deprivation. The Holy Spirit is God's total gift of himself. We receive him, we betray him at our peril, and we rely on him to empower right actions and true words. When I was longing for true faith to make sense of my life, I was not the least bit interested in ecstatic raving; but there was a passion burning within me that I had never known. And that passion, ultimately, was to be saved—saved first of all from all the things that do not satisfy in this world, and saved at last for a kingdom that will have no end. This past, present, and future saving is the subject of our next chapter.

6

Are You Being Saved?

❧

You may have had an experience of being asked, "Are you saved?" Different Christians who ask this question have different understandings of how the process may unfold for you if your reply is "no," or if the question itself baffles you. If your answer is "yes," you might still be missing something they are looking for. Maybe you hear the question with a particular word emphasized: "Are *you* saved?" Or "Are you *saved*?"

The Bible and Christian tradition makes a bigger deal about the *saved* than the *you*: Jesus saved and Jesus saves, once and for all. "When Christ had offered for all time a single sacrifice for sins he sat down at the right hand of God" (Hebrews 10:12). In the old language of the *Book of Common Prayer*, the priest prays at the Holy Eucharist:

All glory be to thee, Almighty God, our heavenly Father,
for that thou, of thy tender mercy, didst give thine only
Son Jesus Christ to suffer death upon the cross for our
redemption; who made there by his one oblation of himself once offered, a full, perfect, and sufficient sacrifice,
oblation, and satisfaction, for the sins of the whole world.[1]

In short, the world has been saved once and for all. That's
the truth. What Jesus did cannot be repeated. What Jesus did
is not dependent upon me. And yet, I want to experience it.
So, am I saved? If so, how?

And what about God's knowledge? If he knows in advance
that I will or will not be included in the saving work of Jesus,
then why is living in the world necessary? If I am predestined
one way or the other, isn't God just a puppet master? More
generally, how do I live in the world now, as I contemplate
eternal life one day? Shouldn't the question actually be, "Will
you be saved?" or "Are you being saved?"

These questions and many others are the subject of the
Christian doctrines of the atonement, predestination, and
divinization (or sanctification). We lump them all together
as a subject called soteriology (the study of saving). In each
of these areas, however, Christian traditions diverge in ways
that we do not see in some of the earlier doctrines we have
discussed. Here we must allow for what T. S. Eliot calls "hints
and guesses," especially because the doctrines themselves are
ways of processing other doctrines that we have already discussed. For example, the atonement is related to Christology.
How Jesus saves is dependent upon who he is. Predestination
is related to the sovereignty of the triune God: Father, Son,

and Holy Spirit. God is God, and I am not God. Divinization
is the work of the Holy Spirit (pneumatology). I am a new
creature who needs to live as what I am.

What I mean is this: the questions about salvation are
branches of the tree whose roots and trunk are the ancient
creeds of the Church. Hanging onto these branches gives us
life, even while we need to stay connected to the roots and
trunk. These doctrines matter, and they are our subject in
this chapter.

THE CRUX OF THE MATTER

If you come from any one of several church traditions (for
those of you who come from one at all), you may have been
expecting a fuller explanation in chapter 4 of one part of the
authentic teachings about Jesus: the atonement. This loaded
theological word is worth breaking down into parts: at-one-
ment; in Latin, *adunamentum*. Atonement describes how the
work of Jesus reconciles the world to God. What was divided
is reunited. What was estranged is reconciled. The differ-
ences that were present are gone. The wrong or injury done
has been done away with. Atonement is what Jesus's work on
the cross and empty tomb is all about. So what is the authentic doctrine of the atonement?

First, it is important to remember that it was the story
itself of what Jesus did that mattered to the early Church.
The story itself is doctrine. The Apostles' and Nicene creeds
do not tell exactly how we are saved, but that we are saved.
Nonetheless, part of buying into the story worth living and

dying for is understanding in the depth of our hearts something more about it. The atonement describes the effect of Jesus's death on the cross—the event which, paired with the resurrection, was the whole reason Jesus came into the world, and the whole reason why he had to be both God and man.

The atonement is a part of Christian doctrine that cuts deep into the individual heart but is also experienced among the members of the Church together. It is behind every part of the rest of the Church's authentic teachings, and yet not explained in just one way in the Bible. Jesus died for you and for me. That is both powerful and elusive. When we talk about the atonement, then, we are interested in various ideas that get at a deeper truth—namely, Jesus died for me. And for you. To understand the full effect of that profound truth, follow me through a few different ways of approaching this atonement.

In the Western medieval tradition, a very popular account of how Jesus's death has the power to save us is called the "satisfaction" theory, proposed most famously by St. Anselm. Anselm was a scholarly monk who eventually became the Archbishop of Canterbury. His work *Cur Deus Homo* (Why God Became Man) clearly explains his thoughts on the atonement. This work has been deeply influential ever since it was written in the 1090s.

Anselm argues that because the story of human beings has diverged so far from the story of God, a certain restitution needs to be made. As in every criminal justice system in the history of the world, crimes cannot go unpunished. But no sentence is long enough to satisfy the offenses of humanity. As St. Paul says to the Romans: "The wages of sin is death" (Romans 6:23a). But, he continues, "the free gift of God is eternal life in Christ Jesus our Lord" (6:23b). The transition from what we deserve to what we may actually get is what grace is all about, and it is what Anselm wrote about. Only God can satisfy himself for any wrongs done to him. Anselm says that our salvation "cannot come about unless there should be someone who would make a payment to God greater than everything that exists apart from God."[2] Jesus alone, the God-man, is capable of such an offering.

The Protestant Reformation (1517–1600) produced a version of the satisfaction theory called "penal substitutionary atonement." Following Anselm, it insists on what is painfully evident in our lives. We deserve death, because left to our own devices, we choose death. Adam and Eve set the precedent that we cannot help but follow. Jesus hangs in our place on the cross and overcomes what the cross should have done to us. Prophecies about Jesus, particularly in the prophet Isaiah, prepare us to understand his saving work in just this way:

> Surely he has borne our griefs and carried our sorrows; yet we esteemed him stricken, smitten by God, and afflicted. But he was pierced for our transgressions; he was crushed for our iniquities; upon him was the chastisement that brought us peace, and with his wounds we are healed. All we like sheep have gone astray; we have turned—every one—to his own way; and the LORD has laid on him the iniquity of us all. (Isaiah 53:4–6)

This is a strong theme in the story of God and humanity that naturally invites reflection. More than that, it elicits gratitude. God became man and died for me. Me!

There are other theories of the atonement too. One is called the ransom theory (associated with Origen [ca. 185–ca. 254] and other early fathers), and it describes a cosmic trickery of the devil and the forces of darkness. Usually this theory is a minor element in other more elaborate treatments, such as satisfaction or penal substitution. To favor ransom theory over satisfaction theory would make Satan more powerful than death itself. He is not. Death is the final enemy defeated by Jesus on the cross and in the empty tomb. Satan is death's servant. Nonetheless, he is powerful; and he, too, is explicitly defeated by Jesus forever as part of Jesus's saving work. In one famous hymn, St. Thomas Aquinas (1224–1274) wrote:

> Now my tongue the mystery telling of the glorious Body sing, and the Blood all price excelling, which the Gentiles' Lord and King, once on earth among us dwelling, shed for this world's ransoming.[3]

The last thing that the great tempter, Satan, would expect would be for God to humble himself to become human. The humility of God in the atonement shows Satan for what he is: a loser, with no chance of ultimate success.

Another way to think about the atonement is through the moral influence theory (associated with many thinkers from antiquity to the present, including Peter Abelard (1079–1142) and Immanuel Kant (1724–1804). It has practical implications that preach well from the pulpit—namely,

Jesus demonstrated sacrifice that we are called to emulate. But as a stand-alone explanation of the cross, it is lacking. Like the ransom theory, it is a notable minor theme in a larger composition of atonement doctrine. In my tradition we use a prayer on Palm Sunday that reflects this complexity:

> Almighty and everliving God, in your tender love for the human race you sent your Son our Savior Jesus Christ to take upon him our nature, and to suffer death upon the cross, giving us the example of great humility: Mercifully grant that we may walk in the way of his suffering, and also share in his resurrection.[4]

What Christ did should spur us on to act likewise. But the most important thing is what he did for us because of who he is. He is the One who reconciles us to God.

These different accounts have different strengths. And although we are very interested in the how, we are certain of the what. We might think of it this way: I hope that I may never find myself in court, facing a trial. But if I do, I know I will need a good defense lawyer—someone I trust completely. My faith in his or her abilities, my experience of the good work he does for me, my gratitude for his help—these far outweigh understanding the ins and outs of the strategy used to win the case. And yet there is a strategy and it is important, just not as important to the defendant as the victory itself. We do not have to understand the precise way God saves in order to be a part of it. The mystery of our salvation is, in part, hidden in the cross of Calvary.

Second, the cross can never be separated from the empty tomb. Jesus's death saves us because he walked away from it. To focus too narrowly on the mechanism by which Jesus protects us from hellfire risks overlooking what lies on the other side of the death that he has trampled down. As noted above, "The wages of sin is death, but"—and that is an enormous "but"—"the free gift of God is eternal life in Christ Jesus our Lord" (Romans 6:23). When authentic Christian doctrine becomes the story of our lives, we certainly feel how woefully inadequate we are before the ruler of the universe. But we are not motivated simply to buy his life insurance. Theories of the atonement are helpful if they deepen our hope. Knowing that we have been saved from our sin does just that.

PREDESTINATION

When I was a kid, I used to watch the painter Bob Ross on public television. He had famously puffy hair and a beard, and he talked in a sweet, lilting voice. He was a television icon, and his show *The Joy of Painting* was a cultural institution. Each week he picked a new subject to teach people to paint. He described all kinds of possibilities of the artistic imagination: "Let's put a little cloud in this world" or "I think there's a little tree that lives back here." I love Bob Ross. To me, there is a compelling tenderness about him and his method.

But inevitably I would panic at certain moments when I watched Bob Ross paint. He would usually start the show by displaying a finished version of what he was about to teach. He would start out putting on a simple background of sea or sky; but then he would get daring—a giant glob of brown paint smeared right across the middle of the canvas. Every time I would think, *Well, that's it. He blew it. This is going to be the one painting that he is going to have to say at the end, "Oh boy, this one went wrong. I'm sorry. I don't know what happened there."* But it never happened that way in the end. Not ever. Before I knew it, this giant glob of brown paint turned into a tree that blended in with the rest of the forest. It came out exactly as Bob Ross wanted it.

Now, it is not correct by any means to say that God is an eccentric painter (however good). But we do take hope from the fact that whatever happens, however a brown glob of paint gets on the canvas of our lives and on the canvas of the world, it is God's will to transform it into what he wants it to be. In John 9 Jesus is confronted with questions about a man born blind. "Who sinned," his disciples ask, "this man or his parents . . . ?" (John 9:2). Jesus answers, "It was not that this man sinned, or his parents, but that the works of God might be displayed in him" (John 9:3). St. Paul elaborates, "And we know that for those who love God all things work together for good, for those who are called according to his purpose. For those whom he foreknew he also predestined to be conformed to the image of his Son, in order that he might be the firstborn among many brothers" (Romans 8:28–29). All things. I have heard many people quote these very lines to me in moments of great hardship; faithful Christian people who take comfort from them. Despite the pain and suffering that they are going through, people really can come to a place where they trust in God—that in the fullness of time, he will make all things right for them.

In this way, it is comforting that God knows what we are about before we do. God knows what the painting of our lives and the painting of the world is going to look like, when we do not. We may call out to him, "What is that? What are you *doing*? You *ruined* it!" But he has not—and never will. In fact, God has a way of calling out to us, yet leaving us thinking that we were the ones who called out to him first. He leaves us to think that we knew what the painting was supposed to look like when he is the one who revealed it to us. Sometimes we might think we are in the depths of hell, when actually we are on a path to life. It is all in God's loving providence. God knows everything, God has a will for everything; therefore, there is nothing to be afraid of.

As we saw above, St. Paul the apostle and inspired Christian theologian (along with many, many theologians who came after him) uses a word that some have found to be a little bit scary: predestination. This is a word full of all kinds of connotations that actually are the opposite of what Scripture teaches. When the Bible lays this word *predestination* on us, it means that God is at work in us before we realize it. We are in his sights before we are even aware of him. As Article 17 of the famous 39 Articles of the Church of England puts it, "Predestination to Life is the everlasting purpose of God."[5] God is calling us to follow him. Will we obey? A good doctrine of predestination is about how God's grace is active, unwaveringly aiming at communion with us. He has a will for our lives that has existed before we were born. And this fact that God's will for us is fixed for all time is what provides our assurance in being able to say, as Paul does, "If God is for us, who can be against us?" (Romans 8:31).

A great example of how the doctrine of predestination works in a human life is shown in the biblical figure of King Solomon in 1 Kings 3. Solomon's father, David, has died and he has become the king. He has a monumental undertaking ahead of him. He is the one who is going to build the famous temple in Jerusalem. He is the one who is going to bring untold wealth and prosperity to this kingdom. But at the beginning of his reign, he is not quite sure what to do. He is sitting at a holy site at Gibeon, and he has a dream. God talks first. God is the one who reaches out first to Solomon. God is the one who initiates the prayer. God says, "Ask what I shall give you" (1 Kings 3:5). And how does Solomon take it from there? He is not interested in listing material things that he wants—military successes, money, land, palaces, even the temple. He does not wish for his enemies to die or his rivals to be weakened. He begins with a prayer of thanksgiving, listing the things he knows God has already done, reminding himself and acknowledging before God, God's providence over him and over his people. "You have shown great and steadfast love to your servant David my father" (1 Kings 3:6). He then situates himself in the midst of this steadfast love. "You . . . have given him a son to sit on his throne this day" (1 Kings 3:6). And then he says, "And now, O LORD my God, you have made your servant king in place of David my father, although I am but a little child" (1 Kings 3:7). Of course, he is not literally a little child; he is a grown man. But like a child, he is utterly dependent. This is exactly the sort of thing Jesus means when he talks about the kingdom of heaven. We need a childlike sensibility, a childlike obedience and humility, a childlike wonder in the presence of God in order to get what God is doing. Solomon has it.

Solomon reveals on this glorious day, as he sits on his splendid earthly throne, that his heart is not fixed on his own kingdom, but on God's kingdom. The fact remains, however, that he is overwhelmed with his duties. He says that in the midst of the people so numerous that they cannot be counted, there is just so much to do. There is money to be raised. There are a lot of foreign enemies who would like nothing more than to see Solomon and all his people wiped out. There is internal squabbling. There are big projects that he is going to undertake. He needs help. And this is his moment to get it. God asks him what he wants and what does he say? He prays for wisdom. He asks for "an understanding mind," which could just as easily be translated from the Hebrew as "a hearing heart" (1 Kings 3:9).[6] He prays for a hearing heart. And in the Bible, the heart or mind is the seat of being. It is the innermost depth of a human person—the you that God knows better than you do. In my tradition we pray this old Latin prayer, eventually translated into English by Thomas Cranmer, every Sunday:

> Almighty God, to you all hearts are open, all desires known, and from you no secrets are hid: Cleanse the thoughts of our hearts by the inspiration of your Holy Spirit, that we may perfectly love you, and worthily magnify your holy Name; through Christ our Lord. Amen.[7]

What does this prayer reveal about Solomon, about us, and about God's providence? What has God predestined for us? First, we realize that Solomon must already have the very gift he is asking for, or he would not have known to ask for it. A wise man asks for wisdom. Such is life with God, as revealed in the story of Solomon. God has put Solomon in his sights to give him the gift of wisdom because God is already at work stirring that up in him. But notice: Solomon has to ask for what God predestines for him. He has to want what God wants for him. And this reveals to us that although we are predestined to something very glorious indeed, God is not a puppet master. God is going to accomplish his predestined purposes for the world, and through us, when we choose not our own desires, but God's. And this is not just accidental. The way God works is when our heart's desire matches his desire. We see this alignment made manifest in the case of Solomon.

Solomon also reaps benefits that he has not asked for. God declares, "I give you also what you have not asked, both riches and honor, so that no other king shall compare with you, all your days" (1 Kings 3:13). C. S. Lewis puts it this way: "Aim at Heaven, and you will get the Earth thrown in. Aim at Earth, and you will get neither."[8] Solomon aims at heaven and gets the earth thrown in.

Sometimes we do not get the earth thrown in and it feels as if we don't have much of heaven either. In fact, a lot of the time, we find ourselves not choosing God's holy will. Our hearts are badly out of line with the heart of God and we may come to a place where we rightly discover that without God's grace, our heart's desire will never correspond with God's will. It is only by God's continual work in us that we may come to our senses about what it is God wants at all. And for this reason, we find Jesus giving us powerful images of the ultimate separation of righteousness from wickedness. If we reject the sovereign will of God, there are consequences.

THEOSIS

As we explore the creedal affirmation of Jesus's death and resurrection, we want to be able to understand what it does to us. When we ponder God's foreknowledge of our salvation, we need to go further. Truth matters not only because we want to know how God works or what God knows, but what difference his saving work means for me and for you.

We are here so that God can do his saving work in us, and use us to do his saving work in others. To say that we have been saved is also to say that we are being saved. Many Christians, particularly in the Eastern Orthodox and Eastern Catholic traditions, refer to this process as *theosis*, or divinization: becoming like God. Protestants have spoken of these matters in terms of justification by grace through faith alone and sanctification by the Holy Spirit. Roman Catholics have emphasized justification by faith that issues forth in works. *Theosis* describes union with God through Christ and transformation by the grace of God. *Theosis* is inherently about what God has done (justified), is doing (sanctifying), and will do (glorify).

We discussed in chapter 3 how Jesus is one person with two natures, divine and human. These natures were

united, not mixed. Accordingly, our hope for salvation is
eternal union, but not mixture, with the loving God who
made us. The great Elizabethan Anglican theologian Richard Hooker (1554–1600) notes, amid an elaborate exploration of justification and sanctification, "Christ imparteth
plainly himself by degrees."[9] Being saved is receiving the
gift of Christ himself throughout the course of our lives.
Jesus died once and for all for our sins, but we need his
ongoing saving grace as we fall down again and again. As
he saves us now, he saves our whole selves and invites our
whole being into union with him. Salvation is thus not just
an inner state of being—it is faith born out in works in this
life and looking ahead to unending glory to come. It is a
destiny for the body as well as the soul. St. Peter portrays
God's gracious work in this way:

> His divine power has granted us all things that pertain
> to life and godliness, through the knowledge of him who
> called us to his own glory and excellence, by which he has
> granted us his precious and very great promises, so that
> through them you may become partakers of the divine
> nature, having escaped from the corruption that is in the
> world because of sinful desire. (2 Peter 1:3–4)

Our role to play is one of gratitude and humility. St. Paul
says, "Work out your own salvation with fear and trembling,
for it is God who works in you, both to will and to work for
his good pleasure" (Philippians 2:12–13). As we shall discuss
in chapter 8, this process will not be complete until the Last

Day, but it is going on even now. Thus, we have been saved, we are being saved, and we will be saved. All three statements matter, and all three statements are true.

Finally, all of us are saved as individuals, lovingly created to be like no one else who has ever lived; but salvation is not a solitary activity. The psalmist says, "Give judgement for me, O LORD, for I have lived with integrity" (Psalm 26:1 BCP), and "In you, O LORD, have I taken refuge; let me never be put to shame; deliver me in your righteousness" (Psalm 31:1 BCP); but also, "May God be merciful to us, and bless us" (Psalm 67:1 BCP), and "Oh, how good and pleasant it is, when brethren live together in unity" (Psalm 133:1 BCP). We know deep within us that we are not the main characters in the story of the world. Our salvation—however individual it ultimately is—is worked out together with others. We live for God as a recipient of grace offered to all the individuals in the whole company of believers called the Church. Many of us today cannot see the way to consider human interconnectedness. But God makes it clear to us who look and listen. Eastern Orthodox theologian Kallistos (Timothy) Ware puts it this way:

> *Theosis* according to the likeness of the Trinity involves a common life, and it is only within the fellowship of the Church that this common life of coinherence can be properly realized. Church and sacraments are the means appointed by God whereby we may acquire the sanctifying Spirit and be transformed into the divine likeness.[10]

Once again, the biblical and doctrinal lens through which we need to examine this and every claim about salvation is called *grace*. Let us explore it now.

We cannot hide our life from God. God is with us. Why are there those people who "do not believe"? Why would God create a world where we "put ourselves against each other." — Some denying his existence".

7

Guaranteed Grace

~

Sometimes we just want to be left alone, especially when we're sad or ashamed of ourselves. The truth can scare us. When we've done something we shouldn't have done or feel things that seem too complicated to explain to anyone, many of us hide. Adam and Eve did just this after they disobeyed God in the garden of Eden. But God wouldn't leave them alone. And he won't leave us alone either.

John Newton (1725–1807), the writer of the famous hymn, "Amazing Grace," discovered one day that he couldn't hide his life from God. He was a young sailor and slave trader who realized one day that his life was headed away from the kingdom of God. He declared, "I once was lost but now am found."

In modern parlance, he knew that there is no such thing as "personal space" or "alone time" when it comes to how we relate to the Creator of the universe and the sustainer of all life. When we first realize that this is what God is like, it can make us feel—as it did with John Newton—like a wretch. But in a fully flourishing orthodox Christian life, wretchedness has no hold on us for long. Our infinitely loving God moves in and takes control: "'Twas grace that taught my heart to fear," John Newton confesses, but immediately transitions to "and grace my fears relieved."

But what is grace? Many Christians would agree with this definition from the catechism of the 1979 *Book of Common Prayer*: "Grace is God's favor towards us, unearned and undeserved: by grace God forgives our sins, enlightens our minds, stirs our hearts, and strengthens our wills."[1] Put simply, Christians believe in a God who intervenes. The living God: Father, Son, and Holy Spirit is bound up in every aspect of creation and reveals himself in Holy Scripture, in sacraments, and in the natural world. There are religions and philosophies that shy away from such an immanent God, imagining instead a God who sets things in motion and steps away. But if we really take the Bible seriously and dig into it just about anywhere, we will find that the God of Israel, revealed to us in Jesus Christ, is active in history and active in our lives today. This gracious activity is certainly true in the lives of the saints, as we see above in John Newton's life, and in so many others. There is simply nowhere that God is not doing things. There is no event in which he is not involved. Everything that happens in the world is the result of God's activity, even when we do not or cannot perceive his presence. When sin and evil

[handwritten margin note: But he doesn't always intervene]

work against him, he establishes plans to bring blessing out of misery. God simply loves his creation too much to leave it alone, and this is the first principle of understanding God's active, guaranteed grace. He loves the world and he loves you. He desires that you flourish for eternal life, and he has provided the means—literally everywhere—for this to happen.

Grace and truth are always intertwined. In fact, John tells us that when God became man in Jesus, revealing the full glory of the Father, he did so "full of grace and truth" (John 1:14). We see how this works in many different ways in the Old Testament, from God's provision for Adam and Eve after their expulsion from Eden right up through Israel's return from exile in Babylon and the rebuilding of their temple in Jerusalem (Genesis 3–4; Ezra 1–6). God delivers his people from bondage in Egypt, and rains food down upon them even in their disobedience. He gives them a Law to govern themselves in the midst of a broken world, and a rich land to call home (see Exodus and Numbers). At no point is God sitting a cold distance away. He is always teaching his people who he is and how he would have them live. Everything happens because it is his desire to express his transforming love to one people, Israel—and through them, to save the entire world (Genesis 12:2–3).

In Isaiah 55 we learn of God's role in the agricultural cycle; and the prophet likens God's active role in nature with the disseminating of his eternal Word. Isaiah does not say that seeds are planted and forgotten about, left to the cycles of a natural world detached from its source in God. Instead, the natural cycle is God's doing, watering and bringing the snow. God is the one who both gives the "seed to the sower"

and also "bread to the eater" (v. 10). From the beginning to
the end, God is in control. For the farmer to fail to care for
the seeds he has planted or for vandals to rip up what has
been sown are both ways of working against God and his gracious will for a particular patch of earth. God has destined its
fruitfulness and wills the accomplishment of his purpose. So
it is with God's saving grace, which we find in the distribu-
tion of his eternal Word—guaranteed to be found in Scripture and sacraments, but far more prevalent than we could
ever imagine. Ultimately, God's gracious Word is meant to
get deep down inside each one of us and transform us from
the inside out. The same Lord who set the stars in the heavens
is the Lord whose Word is near you, "in your mouth and in
your heart" (Deuteronomy 30:14; Romans 10:8).

SIN AND GRACE

Like Isaiah 55, Psalm 65 (BCP) rejoices in the Lord who never
fails to intervene: "You visit the earth and water it abundantly" (v. 9); "You prepare the grain" (v. 10); "You drench
the furrows and smooth out the ridges" (v. 11). These are
not passive constructions, but active ones: You do it, God.
You are the one. I cannot do it, and it will not happen by
itself. Earlier in that same psalm, we learn that this interven-
ing God deals with our sin in the same way: "Our sins are
stronger than we are, but you will blot them out" (v. 3 BCP).
We confess our sins and are relieved of their burden. Repentance and forgiveness are not passive activities or accidental
occurrences. We know what we must do, and we know what

God does. God is never idle, never far removed, and never capricious or careless.

St. Paul describes the guaranteed gift of God's activity throughout his letters, and most profoundly in his letter to the Romans. In chapter 7 he diagnoses the illness within us all:

> I have the desire to do what is right, but not the ability to carry it out. For I do not do the good I want, but the evil I do not want is what I keep on doing. Now if I do what I do not want, it is no longer I who do it, but sin that dwells within me. (Romans 7:18–20)

Without God's help, I am fighting a losing battle; but what can I do? Sins do not just disappear on their own.

St. Paul knows the remedy—the same active grace prefigured in the stories of his ancestors, now fully revealed in the Messiah. God's grace delivers us from the sin and death that Christ defeated on the cross. For this reason, Paul does not beat himself up or wallow in shame. He has no desire to remain helplessly sick, but rather to rush headlong to embrace the cure, which could not be easier to find. He rejoices, "There is therefore now no condemnation for those who are in Christ Jesus" (Romans 8:1). God did not leave Paul alone, and he will not leave you alone. God will not leave you to the natural consequences of your sin. In fact, you are going to have to fight pretty hard to keep him from making things right. You are going to have to fight, tooth and nail, to keep God off you—to keep him from accomplishing his will of taking your sins away and transforming you into the person with whom he desires to keep eternal company. Paul tells the Ephesians, "In him you also, when you heard the word of truth, the gospel of your salvation, and believed in him, were sealed with the promised Holy Spirit" (Ephesians 1:13). Sealed. You cannot, therefore, accidentally reject God.

Sadly, some people are unable to receive God's gracious offer, and Jesus talks about them in no uncertain terms. The parable of the wedding feast in chapter 22 of Matthew's Gospel may be the best example (compare with Luke 15:15–24). A king, Jesus tells us, decided to throw a lavish dinner for his son. The invited guests decided not to come, thus proving their unworthiness to have been invited in the first place. A new group, also unworthy, is invited instead. By accepting, they become worthy. One guest, however, wants to come on his own terms. He accepts the offer to attend the banquet but wants to set his own dress code. The king declares, "Bind him hand and foot and cast him into the outer darkness. In that place there will be weeping and gnashing of teeth" (Matthew 22:13). The improperly dressed, unexpectedly invited guest chooses his own ejection from the party. As George Mac-Donald says: "There are only two kinds of people in the end: those who say to God, 'Thy will be done,' and those to whom God says in the end, 'Thy will be done.'"[2]

And what is God's will? His will is that we should be saved, which doesn't just mean "one day." For this reason, God doesn't wait until "one day" to offer us his grace and truth, nor does he dole them out randomly or exclusively. We do not just happen to encounter God, nor do we have to know the right people, live in the right part of the world, or have a lot of free time on our hands. His gifts come at no price to us, because they have been won at the ultimate price for Jesus. God has got us in his sights at all times and in all places. He knew us before we were in our mothers' wombs, and he knows us now even better than we know ourselves. He alone knows what we could be and should be, which is a faithful representation of him who made us in his image. Jesus describes the phenomenon of God's active, transforming grace in the parable of the sower:

> "A sower went out to sow. And as he sowed, some seeds fell along the path, and the birds came and devoured them. Other seeds fell on rocky ground, where they did not have much soil, and immediately they sprang up, since they had no depth of soil, but when the sun rose they were scorched. And since they had no root, they withered away. Other seeds fell among thorns, and the thorns grew up and choked them. Other seeds fell on good soil and produced grain, some a hundredfold, some sixty, some thirty." (Matthew 13:3–8)

Here we remember the agricultural language of Isaiah and the psalmist, who insist upon a God who not only makes everything grow, but puts the seeds in place beforehand. And because God knows that we do not always perceive him, hear him, or obey him, he spares no method and excludes no place or time in order to reach us. In Jesus's first example, sometimes we are simply oblivious. In his second example, we realize how some things fire us up in an instant but die down again just as quickly. In the third instance, a great number of gracious acts of God perish because of all of the clutter in our lives.

We put too many things in places that compete for God. And where we have not willingly erected such barriers ourselves, the world has imposed them for us. Thankfully, God does not stop there. He fills every nook and cranny, knowing that somewhere, someday, his Word will have a perfect opportunity to flourish. His grace and truth will get to us, as we respond to his Word.

THE SEEDLIKE WORD

As it happens, the Bible reveals that the seeds Jesus describes in Matthew 13 have a long history. In the Messiah, they become activated, revealing both the inherent emptiness of the lands where they once dwelled, as well as the potential fecundity of every land. Among the many examples from the Old Testament we notice the beautiful Psalm 19, paraphrased in a beloved hymn by Joseph Addison:

> The spacious firmament on high, with all the blue ethereal sky, and spangled heavens, a shining frame, their great Original proclaim. The unwearied sun from day to day does his Creator's power display; and publishes to every land the work of an almighty hand.[3]

The prophet Amos reminds us of the same:

> He who made the Pleiades and Orion, and turns deep darkness into the morning and darkens the day into night, who calls for the waters of the sea and pours them

out on the surface of the earth, the Lord is his name. (Amos 5:8)

When you know to look for it, you see God's activity everywhere. St. Paul makes a much subtler point to the Athenians in his famous speech on the Areopagus, in the book of Acts:

"What therefore you worship as unknown, this I proclaim to you. The God who made the world and everything in it, being Lord of heaven and earth, does not live in temples made by man, nor is he served by human hands, as though he needed anything, since he himself gives to all mankind life and breath and everything. And he made from one man every nation of mankind to live on all the face of the earth, having determined allotted periods and the boundaries of their dwelling place, that they should seek God, and perhaps feel their way toward him and find him. Yet he is actually not far from each one of us, for 'In him we live and move and have our being'; as even some of your own poets have said, 'For we are indeed his offspring.' Being then God's offspring, we ought not to think that the divine being is like gold or silver or stone, an image formed by the art and imagination of man. The times of ignorance God overlooked, but now he commands all people everywhere to repent, because he has fixed a day on which he will judge the world in righteousness by a man whom he has appointed; and of this he has given assurance to all by raising him from the dead." (Acts 17:23–31)

The brilliant philosophers and famous people of Athens have had God's eternal Word in their midst all along, even though they were unable to recognize it. The seeds have been sown without their knowledge, and now, in Christ, it is time for the seeds to sprout. Whatever was really true in Plato or Aristotle was actually God's doing. Whatever glimpse of glory revealed in their unparalleled sculptures has now been revealed in full in the God-man, Jesus. Grace is everywhere. And so is truth.

One of the Church's earliest theologians, St. Justin Martyr (ca. 100–165), made much of the idea of God's grace being a seed sown far and wide. Justin thought of God's activity as the *logos spermatikos*, which means "seedlike word." The word is not only to be found in the dialogues of the philosophers, the plays of the dramatists, or the altars to unknown gods. In fact, it is deeper and wider than that. God's Word is in plain sight, even when we see our faces reflected in a body of still water. God reminds us of his grace—his constant, omnipresent activity—in our own bodies. Justin writes:

> The human figure differs from the irrational animals precisely in this: that man stands erect and can stretch out hands and has on his face, stretched down from the forehead, what is called the nose, through which goes breath for the living creature and this exhibits precisely the figure of the cross.[4]

Human beings were made cross-like. Truth is staring us in the face. Embedded in our very biology is, from the beginning, our destiny to be saved by the blood of Jesus shed on the cross.

But what about the times when we feel badly disconnected from God? We may be naturally predisposed to receive grace, but it feels at times that we are waiting in vain. If, however, God seems absent or capricious, we misperceive. "If I climb up to heaven, you are there," the psalmist declares; likewise, "if I make the grave my bed, you are there also" (Psalm 139:7 BCP). The Word is in each of us and around each of us all the time. Grace, then, is a "go-getter." God's grace is determined to have us, is relentless to transform us, and powerful to spur growth. From God's perspective, the victory of the kingdom of God is sure. By nature, God's grace is surely irresistible; but in our hurt, pain, and confusion, we sometimes try to put barricades in his way.

A SACRAMENTAL UNIVERSE

God is determined that his omnipresent grace is going to have its way with us, revealing his truth. But how? The overwhelming witness of the Christian tradition teaches that grace is imparted to us in sacraments. Not all Christian churches think of sacraments the same way, but a generous, succinct account like this one may serve as a starting point to unify a variety of viewpoints:

> The sacraments are outward and visible signs of inward and spiritual grace, given by Christ as sure and certain means by which we receive that grace.[5]

Elaborated more fully, and in more traditional language:

Sacraments ordained of Christ be not only badges or tokens of Christian men's profession, but rather they be certain sure witnesses, and effectual signs of grace, and God's good will towards us, by the which he doth work invisibly in us, and doth not only quicken, but also strengthen and confirm our Faith in him.[6]

In Greek the term for sacrament is *mysterion*, and the Church throughout time and space guards these mysteries by teaching responsibly about them, by inviting God's people to partake of them, beginning with Holy Baptism. Baptism initiates us into life in the Spirit, and with it comes the privilege of partaking regularly in the other sacrament instituted by the Lord, Holy Communion.

The number and ranking of the sacraments has proved particularly controversial over the centuries, and not just since the Reformation. Are there seven, two, or something in between? Certainly, the vast majority of Christians on earth can agree on the special quality of baptism and communion, as instituted in the pages of Scripture by Jesus himself. But to be too keen to deny the other five, or perhaps to stop at seven, is to minimize the scope of God's active grace. If grace is everywhere, then it cannot be restricted to a list. On the other hand, if grace is guaranteed in at least two places, Christians ought not only to hold these "certain sure witnesses" in the highest esteem, but insist upon using them.

Since grace is everywhere and active, we might come to think of the whole universe as sacramental, and any created thing may have potential to edify. There are no "mere" symbols, but there is in the same way no "mere" tree, "mere" person, or "mere" conversation. God has made everything, and he will use it all to win you for his kingdom. In fact, we believe that God's grace is actually the missing piece of our nature. Grace does not make us something we are not (albeit a better version), but rather what we were meant to be all along. "If anyone is in Christ," Paul says, "he is a new creation" (2 Corinthians 5:17). The new creation does not rubbish the old one, but reveals what the old one was meant to be from the start. The old passes away and the new comes by way of transformation, not disintegration. In this way, grace is like health. When an unhealthy person becomes healthy, the old way is gone and something new has arrived. Truth has replaced falsehood. The healthy person was the unhealthy person, but now acts differently and has a completely new look. The memory of the old remains, but it becomes increasingly distant and foreign. The Holy Spirit, working through the means of grace, transforms us. By grace God changes water, oil, bread, and wine for his purposes; and he changes us too. When we partake of God's grace in the sacraments, our own flesh and souls remain intact even while they are also becoming something completely new, wonderful, redeemed, and lovable. True.

THE CHURCH

The Russian theologian Alexander Schmemann (1921–1983) wrote that we sometimes live behind "grace-proof walls."[7] Unfortunately our church walls can be just as grace-proof and truth-proof as the walls of a secular establishment or a hardened individual heart. And yet, Christians believe in the Church, despite churches' flaws. In the Apostles' Creed we say we believe in "the holy catholic Church," and in the Nicene Creed we say "one holy catholic and apostolic Church."

Here we must dispel a misconception. Occasionally I will hear someone say that Jesus did not come to found a church, or that organized religion works against the ends that Jesus means for us to pursue. Additionally, for some who say and believe in the words of the creeds, "Church" means something purely invisible, rather than anything like religious institutions on earth. But to say that the Church is something unnecessary or only unseen is like saying that the family is unnecessary or only unseen. Families vary in practices (and quality), but family life is not lived in anticipation of an ideal. It is what it is. To say we believe in the family is not to say that any family is perfect or that all of our members are still with us on earth. But it is to say that it has been and still is tangible and visible, and that it matters. Such is the case with the Church. Jesus uses an agricultural analogy: "Abide in me, and I in you. As the branch cannot bear fruit by itself, unless it abides in the vine, neither can you, unless you abide in me. I am the vine; you are the branches" (John 15:4–5). We can't go it alone.

The Church is the place where grace can happen and truth may be received—where a Christian pursues the sacramental life. But what about the "holy" part? Here we could go astray if we detach "holy" from "catholic." Catholic—*kata holos* in Greek—means "pertaining to the whole." Every authentic Christian community is a microcosm of all Christians on earth, even where certain practices vary. And the Church is holy even when members of churches are not. A brief look at one more ancient heresy is helpful here.

Around the year 400, St. Augustine had a particular dispute with a group called the Donatists, who had a flawed view of grace. They said sinful men could not administer valid sacraments. Augustine answered:

> Baptism in the name of the Father and of the Son and of the Holy Ghost has Christ for its authority, not any man, whoever he may be; and Christ is the truth, not any man.[8]

"Christ is the truth." God's grace does not depend upon our worth or the worth of those who mediate it through the sacraments. Once again, orthodoxy is a huge relief. We know we're not perfect, and we know our churches aren't perfect. Augustine, who lived a life of fleshly pursuits before his conversion to Christianity, reminds us that great saints know themselves to be sinners. "Christ Jesus came into the world to save sinners," says Paul, "of whom I am the foremost" (1 Timothy 1:15). Grace is only and always God's work, even when he chooses to work through us. The truth is always his too.

THE BEAUTY OF HOLINESS

Grace makes us holy as members of the Church, even though we often fail to live up to the holiness we have been invited to share. The Bible makes it plain that holiness is beautiful, and beautiful things are a means to the source of all truth and goodness, God himself. Just as doctrine is a signpost on the road to God, so is beauty. We do not worship a painting, for example, just as we do not worship the Nicene Creed. But famous artwork like Van Eyck's *Ghent Altarpiece* or Bach's *St. Matthew Passion*, like the Creed, is venerable—which is to say, it directs our worship to where it belongs.

During a long span of time, the Church misunderstood grace and tried to detach truth and goodness from beauty through a heresy called Iconoclasm. In about the year 730 the Church forbade the display of icons—and, by extension, stained glass, crucifixes, statues, and other sacred items. As scholar Andrew Louth demonstrates, these items and their use were completely taken for granted before an organized campaign was mounted to call them into question.[9] In other words, most Christians never imagined they were doing anything wrong by having depictions of Jesus or the saints, by using incense, or by having ornately decorated gospel books until they were told otherwise.

At the heart of the dispute was the difference between veneration and worship. When I kneel and say a prayer in front of a painting of Jesus, am I praying to the painting? If I sing in a church with stained glass images of medieval saints, am I singing to them or to God? Iconoclasts, or "image breakers," say that if you put an image in front of you, that's where your worship goes. Iconodules ("image lovers") say that that's silly. There is always something beyond what I am looking at, hearing, smelling, tasting, or touching. I love my wife, and when I am away from her, I miss her. If I look at her picture, it awakens my love for her, not for the picture itself. Do I have to have a picture of my wife with me because it is the only way I can love her while we are apart? Certainly not; but it helps. To forbid my use of a picture in the service of appropriate—even holy—admiration of her is therefore absurd.

This same distinction eventually won the day after bitter, violent struggles in the eighth and ninth centuries. In a brilliant dialogue between "Orthodox" and "Heretic," a theologian named Theodore the Studite (729–826) made the case in a little work called *On the Holy Icons*. Theodore argued that venerable earthly things participate in varying degrees in the holiness of God. They always point to something greater and more real. And whether we are fully conscious of it or not, our hearts and minds have no choice but to turn toward the source of holiness when we encounter something venerable. Likewise, the more venerable something is, the more it may participate in the holiness of God. A mildly pretty piece of music may speak to us about God and turn our hearts toward him. But an overwhelmingly beautiful piece may simply knock us out with God's grace. There is plenty of room for varying tastes and preferences, but the same principle holds.

The Seventh Ecumenical Council of 787[10] officially settled the matter of iconoclasm, although it persisted for decades afterward. In fact, this was the last official council of the undivided Church before the Great Schism between East and West. In their last big decision together, Christians chose to welcome God's grace in the beauty of holiness. Unfortunately in certain places and to varying degrees, iconoclasm reemerged during the Reformation.

Mercifully, most Christians across traditions now understand the difference between veneration and worship perfectly well. When we kneel before an image of Christ, we believe we are kneeling before Christ himself. Theodore the Studite notes that an image of Christ, "shares the name of its prototype, as it shares also the honor and veneration."[11] Some churches may still favor clear glass to stained glass or a cross with Jesus on it rather than a plain cross; but few would call someone a heretic on account of these matters. Moreover, Christian doctrine that reminds us that God gives us common grace through beautiful physical objects frees us to find this grace inside or outside a church. Indeed, even things not explicitly presented as Christian may be pointing to truth, as revealed by their beauty and goodness. This is good news for us who, inevitably, can't spend all of our time either in church or in private devotion.

THANKSGIVING

The response to grace, as with any gift, is humble thanksgiving. In some way all prayers, even our desperate pleas, boil down to thanksgiving. As the medieval mystic Thomas à Kempis (ca. 1380–1471) notes:

> God is generous in granting us the grace of comfort; but man does ill in not returning all to God with gratitude. This is why His gifts of grace cannot flow freely in us, because we are ungrateful to the Giver, and do not return them to their Fount and Source. God will always give grace to those who are grateful.[12]

Thomas is not here suggesting that our gratitude earns us grace. Not in the least. And yet, gratitude is the natural response to receiving it. God's grace is not at all like the Hindu idea of karma. God's grace is not justice, but mercy. God's grace is not about giving us what we deserve, but rather what we do not deserve. It is about God's offer to us, despite the fact that the balance is against us, that he is going to even it out and then some. Moreover, if we were truly full of gratitude, the world would look like God's gracious masterpiece.

An illustration from a recent film may clarify this point. In Richard Curtis's 2013 film *About Time*, a young man named Tim discovers he has a supernatural gift. His father, played by Bill Nighy, sits him down and tells him that the men in their family are able to travel in time. They do so by going to a dark space, like a closet, closing their eyes, clenching their fists, and imagining a time in the past that they would like to see play out differently. (Interestingly, they cannot go into the future.) Tim's dad warns him that this gift will not allow him to change the world in significant ways, but only travel along his own timeline to have a second shot at a past mistake. Tim is determined to use this gift to get a girlfriend. His first attempt is a failure. Despite all of his engineered attempts to make the right impression, the girl of his dreams simply isn't into him. It is not meant to be. A second attempt, despite his nearly ruining what seems to be a perfect match, works out just right. Eventually Tim discovers that the only true success to be found in using his time-travel gift is to relive the same day he has already experienced, changing nothing but his own attitude. He decides, in other words, to give in to what we might identify as grace. He realizes he doesn't deserve his blessings and cannot really change things that are meant to be, but he can enjoy the ride, over and over again. He decides that gratefulness, in good times and bad, is the only response to the extraordinary gift he has been given.

If everything is pure gift from a sovereign God, then we should get on with giving thanks, even when we do not understand. In our most terrible suffering, God is active. In the harsh reality of the worst moments of our lives, we can in faith trust that God is determined to bring good out of bad, and to redeem for his glorious ends even the things that seem completely devastating to us. Grace leads us toward a thankful spirit when the Holy Spirit shows his hand in an answered prayer or other help sent our way. Our decision does not evoke a new work of grace on God's behalf, but reveals what has been going on everywhere, all the time. When we long for and ask for grace, we find the whole world lit up with God's truth. "I once was lost," John Newton's hymn again reminds us, "but now am found, was blind but now I see."

8

The Life of the World to Come

～

What will happen to me when I die? Where will I go?

In the last line of the Nicene Creed, Christians make this claim: "We look for the resurrection of the dead, and the life of the world to come." This is a beefed-up version of a similar sentiment that we express in the Apostles' Creed: "I believe in . . . the resurrection of the body, and the life ever-lasting." In both cases, what interests us here is the doctrine of what happens to us. We who believe certain things about

God and what he has done (the focus of most of this book), rest assured of the end (or is it really the beginning?) of our own stories. After all of the things we say to and about God: Father, Son, and Holy Spirit, ancient, orthodox Christian teaching ends with what it all means for me and for you. And what it all means is encapsulated in these famous words from 1 Corinthians 15:52b–53, known to many from Handel's *Messiah*:

> The trumpet shall sound, and the dead shall be raised incorruptible, and we shall be changed. For this corruptible must put on incorruption and this mortal must put on immortality.

We shall be changed.

It is interesting that we do not say in the creeds, "we look to be released from these prisons called bodies that we inhabit, and we will enjoy floating around on clouds in heaven forever." Aside from being a tad wordy, it is simply unbiblical and unfaithful to Christian tradition. We express hope in a particularly embodied eternity. We believe we shall be raised, just as Jesus was raised. We shall have a body—albeit a different kind of body—just as the resurrected Jesus did. And just as Jesus ate and drank and talked to his friends in his resurrected body (Luke 24; John 21), we will feast at the wedding supper of the Lamb in ours (Revelation 19.9). We will live forever with God. Our story and God's story will finally make perfect sense together.

BODIES

We notice subtle changes in our physical bodies as we grow older. Even thirty-five-year-old people can attest that things feel a lot different than when they were twenty-five. Child-bearing changes women's bodies, and all sorts of wear and tear from sports and activities catch up with men (and women) as they exit their most vigorous years. A friend of mine had the misfortune of tearing his Achilles tendon shortly after he turned forty. He lamented to me, "The warranty is up on me." Even people in the prime of youth are laid low with a reminder of their mortality when they come down with a cold. Our bodies let us down. They just do. But the Christian faith teaches us that they are not destined for the trash can. They are destined for eternal upgrades. This is what we're looking for.

St. Paul teaches us, "We know that while we are at home in the body, we are away from the Lord, for we walk by faith and not by sight" (2 Corinthians 5:6–7). We know that our bodies limit us, and our worry about them impedes our faith. For example, when we are sick or suffering, we do not always feel pious or charitable. Alternatively, if we think too much about how good we look, we forget our dependence on God who gave us life. But our bodies are not evil. Jesus himself had a body that he did not treat as alien matter. He used his body to commune with his Father; he feasted and fasted. He prayed. His flesh was tortured, he was wrapped up in a burial shroud, and he walked out of his tomb. Jesus's faith was (and is) entirely embodied, and so is ours. Therefore, "we are of good courage," even though our bodies can be great annoyances to us sometimes (2 Corinthians 5:8). On the one hand, our bodies are vehicles for sin and therefore cause us all sorts of misery. They are so obviously corruptible. On the other hand, just as we can sin with our bodies, we can be blessed in our bodies and do God's work with them. Our bodies may weigh us down sometimes, but they can also lift us up. Just as we can make poor choices about where we take our bodies and how we treat our bodies, we can also make good choices with them that have eternal significance.

We need to go even further with this thought. God has given us our bodies precisely for redemption. We take our whole selves to church to receive the sacraments. We use our eyes to read Scripture. We use our mouths and ears to have edifying conversations. Our bellies welcome good food shared with good company. In this way, what we are looking for in the resurrection of our bodies makes more sense. If our bodies matter now, they will matter then. Jesus did not come to liberate us from our bodies. He came to join us in having one. He suffered and died, and came back to life so that we may do the same. There would have been no point in Jesus having a body—or in even being human!—if our eternal destiny was to float around as a wispy, heavenly ghost. We are creatures, and the best way to understand our eternal destiny—that is, to be Christlike—is to imagine ourselves as the ultimate form of a creature. Put another way, to be like God means to be most ourselves. And God knows our true selves better than we do.

As we began to see earlier, one of the best places in the Bible to look for a rich account of bodily resurrection is 1 Corinthians 15. Here Paul develops the image of the earthly body as a seed for the eventual growth of the heavenly body. Paul builds on Jesus's prophetic words about his own death in John 12:24, "unless a grain of wheat fall into the earth and dies, it remains alone; but if it dies, it bears much fruit." And to Paul, who is always talking about the diversity of the body of Christ, there are all kinds of different seeds besides wheat:

> But someone will ask, "How are the dead raised? With what kind of body do they come?" You foolish person! What you sow does not come to life unless it dies. And what you sow is not the body that is to be, but a bare kernel, perhaps of wheat or of some other grain. But God gives it a body as he has chosen, and to each kind of seed its own body. For not all flesh is the same, but there is one kind for humans, another for animals, another for birds, and another for fish. There are heavenly bodies and earthly bodies, but the glory of the heavenly is of one kind, and the glory of the earthly is of another. There is one glory of the sun, and another glory of the moon, and another glory of the stars; for star differs from star in glory.
>
> So it is with the resurrection of the dead. What is sown is perishable; what is raised is imperishable. It is sown in dishonor; it is raised in glory. It is sown in weakness; it is raised in power. It is sown a natural body; it is raised a spiritual body. If there is a natural body, there is also a spiritual body. (1 Corinthians 15:35–44)

Raised. Unique. Embodied. Glorious. What was weak becomes strong. What was limited by nature becomes freed by grace. That is the hope for eternity that Christians believe to be true.

Here we realize that timeless, orthodox Christian teaching is an enormous relief. Salvation not only means that you get to go on being you, but you get to be the real you. All of the wholesome things you enjoy doing add up to mean something for what comes next. Eternity, like the present, will be relational and substantial. The burial liturgy in many of our churches makes this abundantly clear. In my tradition every funeral starts with a series of anthems taken from key passages of Scripture that reinforce our resurrection hope. My favorite is taken from the book of Job (19:25–27), who in the midst of agony in his earthly life, looks ahead to what comes next:

> As for me, I know that my Redeemer lives
> and that at the last he will stand upon the earth.
> After my awaking, he will raise me up;
> and in my body I shall see God.
> I myself shall see, and my eyes behold him
> who is my friend and not a stranger.[1]

NOT THE HELL YOU THOUGHT IT WAS

There is another curious line in the creeds that we must reckon with. We profess in the Apostles' Creed that Jesus "descended into hell," while in the Nicene Creed the "hell" part seems to have been left out: "he suffered and was buried." In fact, the two creeds say the same thing, but this fact is not obvious.

And it is not obvious because in the English-speaking world, we are all mixed up about hell.

To start, the New Testament uses two different Greek words that are usually both translated as hell. The first, *Hades*, conveys the same meaning as the Hebrew *Sheol*. It is simply where you go when you die—or rather, where you went after you died until Jesus went there and destroyed it. Ancient Israelites began to develop a strong hope for resurrection, but it was always the idea that on the last day, the righteous would come back from Sheol (*Hades* in Greek, *hell* in English). In their thinking, it wasn't an inherently bad or good place, although pious Jews believed that the experience there could be restful, gathered together as one people in the bosom of Abraham (Luke 16:22, 25). This place—Hades—is where Jesus went when he breathed his last breath on the cross of Calvary. To say that he really died means that he went where everyone else who had ever died was—there was simply no other place to go. New Testament writers were very interested in Jesus's descent. Without it, the same destination would await us too. What Jesus accomplished in his death and resurrection gives Christians a different perspective on imprisonment, torture, and torment.

Imagine yourself accused of a crime. You are tried, convicted, and sent to prison. You may or may not have been sent there justly. But if you are going to triumph over the system in the end, what would you do? You could try to escape, and spend your days hatching plots and thinking about what you would do if you could see the light of day again. Or you could use the opportunity you have unfortunately been given for a greater purpose.

There are many examples of famous Christians who became lights in places of darkness, and especially in prisons. Dietrich Bonhoeffer (1906–1945) is one great example from Nazi Germany. He was a highly educated theologian and pastor. He had it all. But he stood up for the gospel against Hitler and National Socialism, and he was eventually executed just at the end of World War II. This may seem a defeat; but his behavior in this abode of death allowed those who eventually went free to understand life differently. Bonhoeffer led prayers and worship, and he refused to despair of God's saving power.

A contemporary of Bonhoeffer's is equally inspiring. Corrie ten Boom (1892–1993) was from a Dutch evangelical family who hid Jews in secret rooms in their home during World War II. When they were caught, Corrie and her family were imprisoned; she and her sister Betsie were eventually sent to a concentration camp, where Betsie would die. Corrie was in hell, and yet she was able to endure. Indeed, she was even able to forgive the cruelty and wickedness that she and her sister faced on a daily basis. Upon receiving word that Corrie's father had died in prison, she scratched on the wall of her cell, "March 9, 1944 Father set free."[2]

In the world's eyes, death is the worst thing that can happen. If no other punishment or form of coercion will let someone have his way with you, he can take away your life. And this is the glorious trickery of the resurrection: the very worst thing that can be done to us turns out to be not just futile, but achieves the opposite effect. It gives life. With her dying breath, Betsie tells Corrie: "We must tell them that there is no pit so deep that He is not deeper still."[3]

Freedom from captivity. Light in darkness. This is Jesus's mission to Hades, the deepest of depths. He did not escape death but sought it out. He descended to this infamous place, and he did there exactly what he had always done from the start of his story with humanity: "The light shines in the darkness, and the darkness has not overcome it" (John 1:5). When Jesus went to Hades, he made it such that no one would ever have to go there again. He destroyed death itself. He also declared that the Church—his body on earth after his return to heaven—would be unconquered by it. "I will build my church, and the gates of hell shall not prevail against it" (Matthew 16:18). The traditional English word Christians use to describe what Jesus did there is "harrowing"—Jesus ripped up the realm of the dead and ruined it forever. In this harrowing, Jesus ministered to everyone who formerly had nowhere else to go (1 Peter 3:19). There was a way out of death itself, even for those who had lived long before the time of Jesus. As Jesus ascended again, his deed proclaimed the one reality of God, described so poetically by Paul:

> For I am sure that neither death nor life, nor angels nor rulers, nor things present nor things to come, nor powers, nor height nor depth, nor anything else in all creation, will be able to separate us from the love of God in Christ Jesus our Lord. (Romans 8:38–39)

The old hell is finished forever. And so if you still want hell, you're going to have to describe it a different way. And you're going to have to choose it yourself as your experience of reality. There is no more underworld to end up in by default.

SHEEP GO TO HEAVEN, GOATS GO TO HELL

Now we consider the second New Testament word for hell, *Gehenna*. This is not the place described in the creeds, nor does it correspond to the vision of life after death in the Old Testament. At the time of Jesus, Gehenna was the name for the pit of burning trash on the outskirts of Jerusalem. Long before that, it had been a place where children were sacrificed to the god Molech (2 Kings 23:10; 2 Chronicles 28:3). For Jews who knew their geography and history, you couldn't conjure a less comfortable or desirable place to be. When, therefore, Jesus wants to talk about life without God—life without truth—this is the word he chooses.

The light can feel impossibly bright if you are used to living in the shadows. Likewise, reality can seem too real if we are used to a pale imitation. This is the state of humanity before Jesus, and this is the problem his coming into the world is designed to solve.

There is a famous story from the ancient philosopher Plato that illustrates the point. In the "Allegory of the Cave," we are invited to think of a group of people living underground. Their experience of light is just a fire burning above and behind them, and all they see are shadows cast onto the wall in front of them. Their lives are spent as a captive audience watching what seems like a puppet show. We are told,

> The prisoners would in every way believe that the truth
> is nothing other than the shadows of those artifacts. . . .
> And if someone compelled him to look at the light itself,

wouldn't his eyes hurt, and would he turn around and flee towards the things he's able to see, believing that they're really clearer than the ones he's being shown?[4]

Now, Plato is talking here about education; but as Christians we see how it maps well onto salvation, heaven, hell, and the work of Jesus. It is a sad fact that people willingly choose misery over joy, just as they choose ignorance over knowledge. Pain can be a more reliable companion than relief. Forgiveness can feel impossible if you are burdened by what you have done. Hell can seem strangely preferable to heaven.

Gehenna appears only in the New Testament; always in the three synoptic Gospels of Matthew, Mark, and Luke; and always on the lips of Jesus. This is Jesus's word for describing life without him. In Matthew 5:22, he says in the context of the sinful fruit of giving in to anger, "Whoever says, 'You fool!' will be liable to the hell [*gehenna*] of fire." In the same discourse—this time discussing lust—he says "it is better that you lose one of your members than that your whole body be thrown into hell [*gehenna*]" (Matthew 5:29; see also Mark 9:43–48). Jesus counsels his disciples not to fear anything of this world, since—to return to Corrie ten Boom—the worst the world can do is kill the body. "Rather," Jesus says, "fear him who can destroy both soul and body in hell [*gehenna*]" (Matthew 10:28; see also Luke 12:5). Lastly, Jesus's opponents face a bitter destiny: "You serpents, you brood of vipers, how are you to escape being sentenced to hell [*gehenna*]?" (Matthew 23:33).[5]

In the end, there will be a separation. For now it is difficult to know exactly who prefers shadows to light; but one day it will become clear. Until then, we are all a bit foolish, like the cave dwellers in Plato's story who have a hard time turning toward the light. We feel we are sometimes being punished with the truth. We hurt for something easy. It feels more natural to work against light and life than for it. We would oddly prefer to burn than to turn. But now that Hades is gone and only one reality remains—life—our ultimate choice lies ahead of us and also reflects back on everything we have ever done. To my mind, no one has ever described this better than C. S. Lewis *in The Great Divorce*. His guide, George MacDonald, lays it out like this:

> "Son," he said, "ye cannot in your present state understand eternity. . . . But ye can get some likeness of it if ye say that both good and evil, when they are full grown, become retrospective. Not only this valley but all their earthly past will have been Heaven to those who are saved. Not only the twilight in that town, but all their life on Earth too, will then be seen by the damned to have been Hell. . . . At the end of all things, when the sun rises here and the twilight turns to blackness down there, the Blessed will say 'We have never lived anywhere except in Heaven,' and the Lost, 'We were always in Hell.' And both will speak truly."[6]

One reality: heaven to some, hell to others.

BACK TO THE GARDEN

It is time to say something about heaven. We have thought a bit already about heavenly bodies, but not at all yet about heaven itself. Both the Apostles' and Nicene creeds teach us that Jesus "ascended into heaven, and is seated at the right hand of the Father." Heaven is where God is. Unsurprisingly, when the God-man Jesus walks the earth, he says that heaven has come near (Matthew 10:7; Mark 1:15; Luke 10:9). In one sense, heaven is here. God's world and ours are intertwined, and there is nowhere in particular to go. And yet, the Church has long taught that heaven is where you (may) go when you die. Both are true, and we now deal with the latter.

You will remember that our hope is in resurrection. Jesus defeated death, and so will we who belong to him. His victory is our victory. A body like his is ours to be had as well. But from our perspective in time, resurrection day is in the future. Until then, those whose bodies we commit to the earth are alive, but awaiting that moment of complete re-creation. For those who die in the love of the Lord, this means being in the place we usually call heaven. But it may be better to call it paradise. Here is the destination Jesus promises to the man hanging next to him on the cross. "Truly, I say to you, today you will be with me in paradise" (Luke 23:43). Today. One day resurrection will come; but today rest comfortably in paradise "where sorrow and pain are no more, neither sighing, but life everlasting."[7] This heavenly life of rest is free from all of the concerns of life, where we enjoy the presence of God the Holy Trinity. Jesus describes this beautifully:

"In my Father's house are many rooms. If it were not so, would I have told you that I go to prepare a place for you? And if I go and prepare a place for you, I will come again and will take you to myself, that where I am you may be also." (John 14:2–3)

TO JUDGE THE LIVING AND THE DEAD

You may be thinking that I skipped over an important thing in our brief examination of hell, and that is judgment. I believe that the best way to think about judgment is to fold it into our thinking about desiring light over darkness and truth over falsehood. But there is a lot of Scripture to reckon with, and we need at least to take a snapshot of the biblical landscape of judgment.

Now, it is a caricature of Scripture to say that Christianity (or Judaism before it) simply teaches that there are good things and bad things, and our deeds are reckoned up accordingly. But in some ways, this view isn't too far off. Again and again, Jesus points to a person's actions as the rotten fruit born of ill will, evil intent, or a bad heart. Matthew 7 is particularly helpful (and tough) in this regard. Jesus admonishes us not to judge others (v. 1), shares the golden rule of doing to others what we want done to us (v. 12), tells us of a narrow gate that leads to life (vv. 13–14), and teaches that good trees bear good fruit and bad trees bear bad fruit (vv. 15–20). We then read this passage:

"Not everyone who says to me, 'Lord, Lord,' will enter the kingdom of heaven, but the one who does the will of my Father who is in heaven. On that day many will say to me, 'Lord, Lord, did we not prophesy in your name, and cast out demons in your name, and do many mighty works in your name?' And then will I declare to them, 'I never knew you; depart from me, you workers of lawlessness.'" (vv. 21–23)

The unity of our actions and our will to do them is essential. We have already discussed this in terms of the Holy Spirit in chapter 5, but we see it here from a slightly different angle. Life with God is dependent upon living his way. Eternal judgment, as we saw in God's judgment of Noah's neighbors in the story of the flood in chapter 2, is essentially God's seeing the reality of our lives for what it is. We either want to serve him (and sometimes do serve him), or we don't want to serve him (but may, for a time anyway, appear to serve him for some other reason). God knows the difference. God alone sees the heart and what it produces. But this judgment should not be a source of anxiety. Healthy reverence, however, is never out of order. "Work out your own salvation with fear and trembling," Paul tells us. Why? "[F]or it is God who works in you, both to will and to work for his good pleasure" (Philippians 2:12b–13). As we noted about the effect of God's grace in chapter 7, God is determined to do his will in and through you. You can fight against it, but if you do, you are putting yourself into an unnatural state. You are calling into service a judge, jury, and executioner that have no choice but to carry out their work. They would much prefer to enjoy your company instead.

It is good news that our judge is Jesus, who "came into the world to save sinners" (1 Timothy 1:15), and who said he will be with us forever (Matthew 28:20; Hebrews 13:5). We, who trust in Christ, need never worry that the final judgment will be unexpectedly awful. Jesus promises us (promises us!): "I am with you always, to the end of the age" (Matthew 28:20). Hebrews 13:5 reminds us of the same: "I will never leave you nor forsake you." I used to say to my students when I taught high school, "If you are prepared, you have nothing to worry about." Here's what St. Paul says:

> But the righteousness based on faith says, "Do not say in your heart, 'Who will ascend into heaven?'" (that is, to bring Christ down) "or 'Who will descend into the abyss?'" (that is, to bring Christ up from the dead). But what does it say? "The word is near you, in your mouth and in your heart" (that is, the word of faith that we proclaim); because, if you confess with your mouth that Jesus is Lord and believe in your heart that God raised him from the dead, you will be saved. For with the heart one believes and is justified, and with the mouth one confesses and is saved. For the Scripture says, "Everyone who believes in him will not be put to shame." (Romans 10:6–11)

We all know that feeling in our gut when we're not pre-pared. We all know when things aren't right. But unlike the result of showing up unprepared for a test in school, simply admitting to the Lord, our judge, that we know we're unprepared is all it takes to pass. Eternal life is not for perfect people, no matter how narrow that gate, but rather for imperfect people who desire to be made perfect in the fullness of time. Living a cycle of repentance and forgiveness in the Church, with an eye always toward final forgiveness, allows us to produce fruit worthy of all the fresh starts we are given. John tells us, "if anyone does sin, we have an advocate with the Father, Jesus Christ the righteous. He is the propitiation for our sins, and not for ours only but also for the sins of the whole world" (1 John 2:1–2). People whose hearts and deeds align this way, despite all their flaws, are those to whom Jesus, our Savior and our Advocate before the Father, says in the end, "Well done, good and faithful servant" (Matthew 25:21, 23).

THE WORLD TO COME

The hope of a new and better world has long been an obsession of humanity. There have been countless theories for the improvement of society. Thomas More's 1516 work *Utopia* (which means "no place") gave rise to a philosophical and literary endeavor that lasts down to the present day. Many thinkers explore its perverse flip side, dystopia, in describing all the ways the world may continue to go wrong. The famous explorers of centuries past all carried hope of a heavenly alternative, along with the more practical concern for new sources of wealth and prestige. The project of colonizing America had "the world to come" at its heart. Take, for instance, the New England city of New Haven, Connecticut, home to Yale University. Haven is another word for "heaven"—a safe place of rest and refreshment. The Puritans laid out this "New" Haven on the other side of the Atlantic in a collection of perfect city squares—a theocratic foretaste of the rule of Christ in the New Jerusalem in Revelation 21.

But human beings have not succeeded in creating a new world. "Our citizenship is in heaven," Paul tells the church at Philippi (Philippians 3:20). He elaborates to the church at Rome:

> For I consider that the sufferings of this present time are not worth comparing with the glory that is to be revealed to us. For the creation waits with eager longing for the revealing of the sons of God. For the creation was subjected to futility, not willingly, but because of him who subjected it, in hope that the creation itself will be set free from its bondage to corruption and obtain the freedom of the glory of the children of God. For we know that the whole creation has been groaning together in the pains of childbirth until now. And not only the creation, but we ourselves, who have the firstfruits of the Spirit, groan inwardly as we wait eagerly for adoption as sons, the redemption of our bodies. For in this hope we were saved. Now hope that is seen is not hope. For who hopes for what he sees? But if we hope for what we do not see, we wait for it with patience. (Romans 8:18–25)

The world is broken and we can't fix it; but we care for this old world because of God's love for it, and his promise to renew it. We conserve what we can, like Robinson Crusoe salvaging his wrecked ship. We sub-create, in partnership with the true artist. We are subcontractors under the authority of the master builder. Christian truth does not teach us that this world does not matter because we are going to escape it one day. Jesus teaches us to pray, "Thy kingdom come, Thy will be done on earth, as it is in heaven" (Matthew 6:10 KJV) This world matters precisely because it is imperfect and God wants to make it right. The book of Revelation gives us a clear picture:

> I saw the holy city, new Jerusalem, coming down out of heaven from God. . . . And he who was seated on the throne said, "Behold, I am making all things new." (Revelation 21:2, 5)

In the Apostles' Creed we profess belief in "the resurrection of the body, and the life everlasting," and in the Nicene we say somewhat more elaborately: "We look for the resurrection of the dead, and the life of the world to come." Clearly we're not just talking about floating off to the stars. As N. T. Wright describes it:

> Resurrection itself then appears as what the word always meant, whether (like the ancient pagans) people disbelieved it or whether (like many ancient Jews) they affirmed it. It wasn't a way of talking about life after death. It was a way of talking about a new bodily life after whatever state of existence one might enter immediately upon death. It was, in other words, life after life after death.[8]

THE END IS THE END

We are sinners in need of redemption. Jesus died for us and rose again that "whoever believes in him may not perish but have eternal life" (John 3:16). For Christians, every Sunday is a celebration of this truth. It is therefore also a celebration of our own hope of life beyond the grave.

I began this book with a description of a very special service in my tradition and others called the Great Vigil of Easter. It is a long service, and for centuries would have been the primary time of year for new, adult converts to finish their instruction in the faith and to be baptized. For these new Christians, it was new life. For the rest of the community, it was looking ahead to the consummation of God's love for the world. To this day, the Church sits in darkness, looking back on all of the stories of God's saving love, situating each individual in the story of God's redemption, and remembering one more important piece of the story. God may have trampled down death by dying on the cross, descending to Hades, and then returning to heaven, but God's work isn't finished.

A moment ago we thought about the final judgment. That judgment comes when what we have been looking for comes into sight. "He will come again in glory," the Church has said in one voice since the year 325. Everything depends on this event. When John reveals the vision God has given him of new creation, it hangs on the promise Jesus puts in his ear: "Surely, I am coming soon" (Revelation 22:20). Here we are, more than two thousand years after God became man. Here we are, two millennia after death died, the Holy Spirit came, and the Church was born. Here we are, all these years later, living on grace and trusting in the promises made to countless generations of spiritual ancestors. There is no fully adequate theory to describe when or how the second coming of Jesus will happen. A whole cottage industry has tried and failed to own space that simply isn't for sale. Instead, Christian truth simply points us to the same place where St. John the Divine found himself on the island of Patmos, thinking through all of these things, and concluding with one simple prayer:

Amen. Come, Lord Jesus (Revelation 22:20).

9

Amen

～

That summer of 2001, when the buildings fell and my faith
was uncertain, worship brought me back to understanding the truth and why it mattered. Christians sometimes use
the Latin expression *lex orandi lex credendi*—"the law of praying is the law of believing"—to reflect on our life of worship
and service. And if "law" is an unhelpful word here, we may
just as well leave it out: praying is believing and believing is
praying. The creeds themselves are pieces of liturgy. None of
the doctrine stuff we have attempted to approach in this book
would mean anything outside of the context of worship. This
is so because humans are made to worship. In chapter 32 of
the book of Exodus, ancient Israel is so desperate to identify
an object of worship that they fall into idolatry before Moses
comes down from the mountain. They believed that God was

absent, and in their confusion, they gave themselves over to the wrong thing: a golden calf. In the absence of truth, we too will settle for lies.

I needed help to realize that right belief is never detached from the right offering of thanks and praise. I needed to learn that truth is just as much an offering to God as a property of God. And I needed to find the Church, where proper worship on this side of eternity takes place. If this book has inspired anything in its readers, my great hope is that it would be a prod to make or strengthen ties to a church. And the thing that Christians do together as the Church is called prayer. Of course, we may pray individually and privately. Our work in the world may be (and should be) done prayerfully. We pray in moments of desperation and in moments of exhilaration. Sometimes we pray very specifically, and at other times "the Spirit himself intercedes for us with groanings too deep for words" (Romans 8:26). But as a body, we pray in common. This holy work ensures that it is not my truth or yours, but the life-giving gift of a loving God. And ultimately this gift is the only thing that makes sense of other kinds of prayers too. How else will I know whether I am bowing down to a golden calf? How else, but with the people of God in the Church, will I know that my faith is not in my god, but in the one true God.

THE END OF PRAYER

The word *Amen* is the last word of both prayers and creeds. It is often sung at the end of a hymn as well. It is an old biblical word, which made its way into English from Hebrew and then Greek. Jesus uses it a lot, often at the beginning of his teachings. We often miss this usage, because it is translated as "truly," or in older English, "verily."[1] Saying "Amen" indicates assenting to the truth. It is a humble gesture of giving myself over to authority outside of myself. A person who says "Amen" is someone who is praying the truth. It is through Jesus, the Son of God, "that we utter our Amen to God for his glory" (2 Corinthians 1:20). It is anything but a formality or a throwaway term.

"Amen," therefore, is the end of prayer, in more ways than one. *End* is a word with two meanings. On the one hand, it means the last word in a sequence. After we say "Amen," we're done saying what we want to say. But "Amen" is also an "end" in the sense of a goal. We talk about a "means to an end." An end, in this case, does not simply mean the last thing, but the thing that everything else has been leading toward.

Think of going to a movie. Let's say that the projector breaks 1 hour and 50 minutes into the film—just ten minutes from "The End." We may be able to say that we've seen the movie. We know what it's about and it may have moved us in certain ways. But it is impossible to assent to its complete quality. And in fact, at the end of a really great movie, you might even find yourself moved to shout out "Amen!" But the point is, the end is the end. When the credits roll, whatever has just happened before the screen went black casts light or shadow back onto everything that came before. Without "The End," the beginning and middle are woefully incomplete.

The Amen in prayer and song—which are how we express Christian truth—is an affirmation of the whole endeavor of a life of faith. There is nothing piecemeal about truth. It is a packaged set. It is a Shakespearean five-act, rather than a detachable soliloquy. The Victorian poet Christina Rossetti has a poem called "Amen," in which she writes:

> It is over. What is over?
> Nay, how much is over truly:
> Harvest days we toiled to sow for;
> Now the sheaves are gathered newly,
> Now the wheat is garnered duly.
> It is finished. What is finished?
> Much is finished known or unknown:
> Lives are finished; time diminished;
> Was the fallow field left unsown?
> Will these buds be always unblown?
> It suffices. What suffices?
> All suffices reckoned rightly:
> Spring shall bloom where now the ice is,
> Roses make the bramble sightly,
> And the quickening sun shine brightly,
> And the latter wind blow lightly,
>   And my garden teem with spices.[2]

The Amen of prayer and song and doctrine is a provisional one, and often repeated. We began this book with T. S. Eliot's insistence that life is cyclical, and life is prayer. But in all the seasons of our lives, God's changeless truth is there. Our frequent utterances of "Amen" to God bear witness to God's final Amen to us. When terrorists attack, when our minds are clouded by doubt, when we enjoy peace and prosperity, and when our hearts are full of joy: Amen is our final word.

And yet, as Rossetti asks in her poem, "What is finished?" One thing ends, and another always begins. For now. Being a person for whom truth matters, therefore, is to be always exploring with the end in mind, but not always in sight.

A SUITCASE WITH TOO MANY CLOTHES

To be able to say "Amen" to the whole of Christian doctrine, however, requires a settled commitment of faith. You may like one bit better than another. I know I do. But I am not asked for my opinion. I am asked for my obedience. And when I give it, I experience freedom.

Choosing obedience over my particular preferences, however, means living with something of a mess and an ongoing need of help. A professor of mine used to say that Christian doctrine is like a suitcase that is just a little bit too small for all of the stuff you have to put in it. When you cram a shirtsleeve back in on one side, you will find a sock or a handkerchief hanging out the other side. You may need to find a friend or two to sit on it for you to close it so that you can carry it about. Saying "Amen," therefore, does not mean you have to have everything completely figured out.

Saying "Amen" also does not mean you will not grow and change in your understanding of certain doctrines, even while you say the same words of the same creeds, partake of the same sacraments, and read the same Bible. You may pray in various ways throughout your life. You may even experience common prayer in one denomination or communion and then find yourself moved to another. Few Christian lives are lived without what we might cautiously call progress. God forbid we call it regress. We are always moving. And the way that the truth affects us ought to mean that we are moving toward God and being conformed to the image of his Son instead of moving away from him. But we all face forks in the road. Sometimes we make a wrong turn and find ourselves desperate and stuck. Sometimes we are careless and find ourselves moved along in a bad direction by others. Christian truth lived in community puts the "Amen" back on our lips and in our hearts. Sometimes we need someone to pack the suitcase for us, put it in our hands, and send us on our way. This has been my experience over the years.

CANA OF GALILEE

Humans are both too fragile and too complex to leave questions of truth outside of the context of worship. Without weekly or even daily "Amens" to God's truth, it slips away from us. But inside of a life lived in a rhythm of prayer, life outside of church can also embody the Amen, the final truth of the kingdom of heaven which has come near.

In chapter 3 I talked about a famous passage from Fyodor Dostoevsky's *The Brothers Karamazov*. I will now talk about another powerful but not-so-famous one. In my earlier example we met Alyosha, a novice monk, who defends the truth of the gospel against his atheist brother, Ivan. Alyosha has been told prophetically that he is not going to be a monk after all. His spiritual mentor has died, and he now faces the world in a new way. He must walk through his old house of prayer one final time. When he does, he realizes the permanent effect of countless "Amens" prayed alongside his brother monks. Alyosha comes in from dealing with the mess of his family and passes straight through a vigil being kept around the body of his spiritual elder, Zossima. One of the men is reading aloud from Scripture—John 2, the story of Jesus's first miracle, turning water into wine at the wedding feast at Cana. Alyosha has unwittingly been transformed like the water, a living sacrament. He bears witness to the great "Amen" of God to creation. As he leaves the monastery and reenters the world, we are told:

> Over him hung the heavenly dome, full of quiet, shining stars, hung boundlessly. . . . With each moment he felt clearly and almost tangibly something as firm and immovable as this heavenly vault descend into his soul. Some sort of idea, as it were, was coming to reign in his mind—now for the whole of his life and unto ages of ages. He fell to the earth a weak youth and rose up a fighter, steadfast for the rest of his life, and he knew it and felt it suddenly, in that very moment of his ecstasy.[3]

A life lived within the boundaries of truth creates this same kind of immense sense of space and freedom. As a young man I decided to say "Amen" to this life. I invite you to do the same.

CONCLUSION: OPEN TO INTERVENTION

A person addicted to drugs or alcohol may have a lot of family members and friends praying and working for their deliverance from substance abuse. They may even stage an intervention, taking turns describing to the addict all the ways he or she has hurt others as a result of a monomania for intoxication. The goal of such a conversation is that the addict would begin a process of transformation, to turn from his or her ways and be delivered from the thing that is robbing him or her of a better life. In these instances, friends and family do not just suddenly want to help. It is usually the product of years of hurt and longing. But the intervention is the moment to say to an addict, "Do you want freedom? Do you want healing? It is available in a thousand different places, and we want to show you how you can have it."

God wants you to be transformed, healed, and saved by his grace. His truth draws you to him like a magnet. It has been on offer forever, and it remains today the greatest bargain of all time. You do nothing but assent. You say "Amen"— not just once, but throughout your life of faith. The true God who is never of your own making, and who may frustrate you before he comforts you, will never leave you alone. If he did, he would not be the God of love. God has planted his grace and revealed his truth in every part of your life, from the Bible that you hold, to the sacraments you take, from the stars in the heavens, to the reflection of your own face looking back at you. Give in. God is waiting.

And that's the truth.

Endnotes

Chapter 1

1. Rowan Williams, *Writing in the Dust: Reflections on 11th September and Its Aftermath* (London: Hodder & Stoughton, 2002), 5.

2. Ibid., 9.

3. T. S. Eliot, "The Dry Salvages," *The Four Quartets* in *The Complete Poems and Plays: 1909–1950* (New York: Harcourt, Brace and Company, 1958), 136.

4. Eliot, "Little Gidding," *The Four Quartets*, 139.

Chapter 2

1. T. S. Eliot, "Burnt Norton," *The Four Quartets* in *The Complete Poems and Plays: 1909–1950* (New York: Harcourt, Brace and Company, 1958), 119.

2. Zephaniah is the ninth of the twelve books of the "Minor Prophets" found toward the end of the Old Testament. It is a marvelous and rarely read book that I commend to you.

3. This is what we mean in the creeds when we say that Jesus "descended into Hell" or "descended to the dead." More on this strange and important statement in chapter 8.

4. See, among other things, "The Confession of the Arians, Addressed to Alexander of Alexandria," in *Christology of the Later Fathers*, ed. and trans. Edward Hardy (Louisville: Westminster John Knox Press, 2006), 332–34.

Chapter 3

1. T. S. Eliot, "The Dry Salvages," *The Four Quartets* in *The Complete Poems and Plays: 1909–1950* (New York: Harcourt, Brace and Company, 1958), 136.

2. One of the most important passages in the New Testament for early Christology is Jesus's exegesis of Psalm 110:1 in Matthew 22:41–46, in which the king (David) has the Lord invite "my lord" (that is, David's king) to sit at God's right hand.

3. "The Tome of Leo," *Christology of the Later Fathers*, ed. Edward R. Hardy, trans. William Bright (Louisville: Westminster John Knox Press, 2006), 363.

4. Ibid., 365.

5. "The First Letter of Nestorius to Celestine," *Christology*, 348.

6. St. Cyril of Alexandria, *On the Unity of Christ*, trans. John Anthony McGuckin (Crestwood, NY: St. Vladimir's Seminary Press, 1995), 59.

7. "The XII. Anathematism of St. Cyril Against Nestorius," *The Nicene and Post-Nicene Fathers*, Second Series, Vol. 14: *The Seven Ecumenical Councils of the Undivided Church*, ed. Henry R. Percival (Peabody, MA: Hendrickson Publishers, 2012), 206.

8. "The Chalcedonian Decree," *Christology*, 373.

9. "To Cledonius against Apollinaris (Epistle 101)," *Christology*, 215.

10. Fyodor Dostoevsky, *The Brothers Karamazov*, trans. Constance Garnett (New York: Signet, 1957), 229.

11. Ibid., 233.

12. Ibid., 235.

13. Athanasius, "On the Incarnation," trans. Archibald Robinson in *Christology*, 107. This is a notoriously controversial phrase to translate. Compare "He, indeed, assumed humanity that we might become God" in the translation by a religious of C.S.M.V. (Crestwood, NY: St. Vladimir's Seminary Press, 1996), 93.

Chapter 4

1. Paul Tillich, "Theology of Education," address at the Symposium, October 1956, Celebrating the 100th Anniversary of St. Paul's School, https://www.sps.edu/ftpimages/36/misc/misc_93016.pdf.

2. Ibid.

3. Via the Holy Spirit, via the Word of God. See chapter 5.

Chapter 5

1. The common biblical term *heart*, rendered from the Greek *kardia*, means something more like "the depth of one's being." *Gut* or *guts* may signify this better in modern American English.

2. Jerome, "The Dialogue Against the Luciferians 7," *Ancient Christian Commentary on Scripture, New Testament II: Mark*, eds. Thomas C. Oden and Christopher A. Hall (Downers Grove, IL: InterVarsity, 1998), 10. Compare with Romans 6:3–5.

3. Compare Exodus 3:2. The angel of the Lord is in a burning bush, and the angel gives way to the voice of the Father: "I am who I am," echoed by Jesus throughout the Gospel according to John, where Jesus talks about the Holy Spirit as his replacement: "a new advocate" or "comforter."

4. C. S. Lewis, *The Lion, the Witch, and the Wardrobe* (New York: Harper Trophy, 2000), 80.

5. Rowan Williams, *The Lion's World* (Oxford: Oxford University Press, 2012), 70.

6. C. S. Lewis, *The Screwtape Letters* (New York: Harper Collins, 2001), 76.

7. Jeremy Taylor, *Holy Living and Holy Dying*, in *Jeremy Taylor: Selected Works*, ed. Thomas K. Carroll (New York: Paulist Press, 1990), 447.

8. Matthew 1:18, 20; more famously Luke 1:35.

9. For some very concise history, see Timothy Ware, *The Orthodox Church* (New York: Penguin, 1997), 49–52.

10. Justin Holcomb, *Know the Heretics*, KNOW Series (Grand Rapids: Zondervan, 2014), 85. Holcomb is discussing what he calls "the most intellectually well-developed form of Modalism," which is Sabellianism. See 77–86.

Chapter 6

1. *The Book of Common Prayer* (New York: Church Publishing, 1979), 334.

2. Anselm, "Why God Became Man," in *Anselm of Canterbury: The Major Works*, eds. Brian Davies and G.R. Evans; trans. Janet Fairweather (Oxford: Oxford University Press, 1998), 319 (2.6).

3. *The Hymnal 1982* (New York: Church Publishing), 329.

4. *The Book of Common Prayer* (New York: Church Publishing, 1979), 272.

5. Ibid., 871.

6. Unfortunately for Solomon, he lost his wisdom at the end of his life. His fervor for the Lord at the dedication of the temple (1 Kings 8) gives way to his overindulgence in pleasures of the flesh

and the worship of the gods of his many wives (1 Kings 11). His great kingdom then falls apart upon his death (1 Kings 12 ff).

7. *The Book of Common Prayer*, 355.

8. C. S. Lewis, *Mere Christianity* (New York: Harper One, 2001), 134.

9. *The Laws of Ecclesiastical Polity* V.lvi. (London: JM Dent & Sons, 1907), 231.

10. Timothy Ware, *The Orthodox Church* (London: Penguin, 1997), 237–38.

Chapter 7

1. *The Book of Common Prayer* (New York: Church Publishing, 1979), 85.

2. Quoted in C. S. Lewis, *The Great Divorce* (New York: Harper Collins, 2001), 75.

3. *The Hymnal 1982* (New York: Church Publishing Inc.), #409.

4. Justin Martyr, "First Apology, 55," in *Early Christian Fathers*, ed. Cyril C. Richardson (New York: Touchstone, 1996), 278.

5. "Catechism," in *The Book of Common Prayer* (New York: Church Publishing, 1979), 857.

6. "Article XXV. Of the Sacraments," The Articles of Religion, in *The Book of Common Prayer* (1979), 872.

7. Alexander Schmemann, *For the Life of the World* (Crestwood, NY: St. Vladimir's Seminary Press, 1963), 127.

8. Augustine, "The Letters of Petilian, the Donatist," in *The Nicene and Post Nicene Fathers*, vol. 4, ed. Philip Schaff (Peabody, MA: Hendrickson, 2012), chapter 24.57, 545.

9. Andrew Louth, *Greek East and Latin West: The Church AD 681–1071* (Crestwood, NY: St. Vladimir's Seminary Press, 2007), 42–45.

10. "The Seventh Ecumenical Council" in *The Nicene and Post Nicene Fathers*, vol. 14, ed. Henry R. Percival (Peabody, MA: Hendrickson, 2012), 521–87.

11. Theodore the Studite, *On the Holy Icons*, trans. Catherine P. Roth (Crestwood, NY: St. Vladimir's Seminary Press, 1981), 52.

12. Thomas à Kempis, *The Imitation of Christ*, trans. Leo Sherley-Price (New York: Penguin, 1952), 81.

Chapter 8

1. *The Book of Common Prayer* (New York: Church Publishing, 1979), 491.

2. Corrie ten Boom, with Elizabeth and John Sherill, *The Hiding Place* (Grand Rapids: Chosen, 2006), 170.

3. Ibid., 227.

4. Plato, *Republic* (514a–520a) in *Plato: Complete Works*, ed. John M. Cooper, trans. G. M. A. Grube (Indianapolis: Hacket, 1997), 971–1223.

5. Philip S. Johnston, "Gehenna," *The New Interpreter's Dictionary of the Bible*, Volume II (Nashville: Abingdon, 2007), 531.

6. C. S. Lewis, *The Great Divorce* (New York: Harper Collins, 2001), 69.

7. *The Book of Common Prayer*, 499; see also Revelation 21:4.

8. N. T. Wright, *Surprised by Hope: Rethinking Heaven, the Resurrection, and the Mission of the Church* (New York: Harper One, 2008), 151.

Chapter 9

1. Compare Matthew 5:26, among many other examples, in a modern translation and the King James.

2. Christina Rossetti, "Amen," *Selected Poems* (London: Penguin, 2008), 34.

3. Fyodor Dostoevsky, *The Brothers Karamazov*, trans. Constance Garnett (New York: Signet, 1957), 362–63. I am grateful to Bryan Owen for showing me how wonderful this passage is.